values first

values first

HOW KNOWING YOUR
CORE BELIEFS
CAN GET YOU THE LIFE AND
CAREER YOU WANT

LAURA EIGEL, PH.D.

HOUNDSTOOTH
PRESS

Names and identifying characteristics of some individuals have been changed. Some dialogue has been recreated.

Dedicated to my sister Michelle.

Contents

Prologue

WEARING A BORROWED WHITE BANANA REPUBLIC BLAZER, I was feeling queasy but prepared as I walked into the job fair. I had just defended my dissertation in graduate school and borrowed $300 from my parents for a flight and registration fee to attend a conference in Los Angeles. I stayed with my childhood best friend, Helena, who lived in Pasadena. Helena gifted me the white blazer to wear for my interviews; her mom had bought it for her, and she'd never worn it. The blazer still had the tags on it when she offered it to me (a price I could never afford on my own). Putting it on, I hoped it magically covered my anxiety and turned it into casual confidence.

I was feeling very official with my white blazer and newly minted PhD. I had a few meet-and-greets lined up and went to the conference to apply for more positions. There was one job that I had chosen not to pre-apply for. It was for a small consulting firm outside of my hometown. They were looking for new PhDs with specific experience, and while I had the credentials, I didn't have the experience. I'd done some consulting work in my graduate school, but never the exact things that were written in the job description. I felt like I could do the job and figure it out along the way. I loved learning, diving in. But I didn't meet the objective criteria, so I didn't apply.

At the job fair, each employer had a box, and if you hadn't pre-applied for the position, you put your paper resume in the box to apply. There was a big piece of furniture with slot numbers representing the companies. I looked at this tall grid marked for employers. *Would one of these companies be my first employer? Would I really get a job here? Would I get second interviews onsite? Would I be able to make it through the day without throwing up?*

My nerves were getting the better of me, so I decided to make a lap around the conference. Getting the lay of the land, getting familiar with my surroundings, and doing some people-watching have always been ways for me to calm myself a bit. I walked around the conference, seeing people rushing into rooms to hear a talk, seeing old friends reuniting with each other, and spying on others who were awkwardly networking.

After people-watching, I came back around to the job fair area and stared at the resume boxes. There I was with the fancy faux-leather portfolio my father had given me to put my newly printed resumes in, standing there looking at the boxes. To say I was nervous would be an understatement. Opening my portfolio, I reviewed the notes I took—which box numbers did I want to put my resumes in? One copy of my resume hesitantly went in the box for a gig in Oklahoma, and another for a job in New Jersey.

With a quick scan of the boxes, I found it. The box for the company I had chosen not to apply to. Because, you know, I wasn't qualified for that one. I looked behind me and caught a glimpse of myself in the mirror. The white jacket gleamed back at me.

In my mind, I heard the voice of my professor from my program evaluation class: "After this class, you'll know how to evaluate anything. You'll be able to go into any situation because you'll know what to do, even if you've never done it before."

With my resume in hand, I stared down the box. I love to learn, I can figure this out, I thought. In that moment, centering in on what I knew was true—that I loved to learn and be challenged—I knew what I had to do.

I stared at my resume, then the box, then the resume, then the box; I held my breath and quickly shoved my resume in... Then I ran out of there as quickly as I could so I couldn't change my mind—such a rule breaker, applying for a job that I wasn't qualified for.

Guess which job I ended up getting? You know, that one—the one I almost didn't apply for.

This is a book about knowing what you value—and using that to get the life and career you want.

Put your resume in the freaking box.

Introduction

IN BUSINESS AND IN LIFE, WE ARE OFTEN TOLD THAT THE ideal type of leader is someone with the right executive presence and charisma to motivate teams. We are sold the image of a leader as someone who dedicates their whole life to work, going above and beyond everyone else, often being the loudest person in the room.

That type of leadership didn't work for me. I'm guessing it doesn't work for you, either.

I've spent my career studying, working with, and building the capability of great leaders in all sizes of organizations, from small businesses to Fortune 500 companies. In my research, I have found that what makes a true leader isn't how loudly you command a room, but how authentically you show up as yourself in your values.

In this book, I share my experience with being the quiet one in the room, amongst lots of ambitious, extroverted leaders. Throughout my career, my introversion has been both a strength and an obstacle to overcome. I studied personality and temperament in graduate school. I'm not here to test you. I'm not analyzing you. I'm not here to tell you what the perfect profile is for a leader (hint: there isn't one).

I'm here to tell you about what I've learned in my two decades of studying and working with high-performing leaders. I want to tell you that there is no one way to be a great leader, except to lead with your authentic style.

When you show up authentically, centered in your values, you'll be more successful. I know this to be true for myself. You will learn how to do this through the Values First™ Framework.

This is the framework that I've used to build boundaries and create a team culture to motivate others to achieve success, while leading as my authentic self. It is the framework that I use to coach executives to do the same.

Throughout the book, I'll guide you through the Values First Framework. You'll learn through my experience, and I'll challenge you to do some serious self-reflection and action-taking along the way. The framework consists of six parts:

Here's what you'll accomplish in each section of this book using the framework:

Values First Framework from The Catch Group

- **Values First.** Dig into what matters most to you and set the foundation of your core values. You'll also get clarity on what living those values looks like uniquely to you.

- **Audit Time.** Review your time to see where your values do and don't show up in your life and learn how to use your values to make difficult decisions at home and at work.

- **Life Boundaries.** Set your Values First priorities to create the boundaries you need to truly live the life that you want and create a system for keeping those boundaries in place.

- **Uplifting Others.** Find the support you need from peers and mentors to keep your boundaries intact and learn strategies to model your values with your team by building a Values First culture as a leader.

- **Experiencing Conflict.** Create a plan now so when conflict arises with yourself or your team, you can easily know what to avoid and how to move forward in alignment with your values.

- **Sustaining Values.** Build an action plan to live your values and boundaries for the long haul.

That's your full Values First action plan, and what you'll go over in each section. To get the most out of this book, here's what you need to do:

- Download the free Values First workbook at www.the-catchgroup.com/valuesfirst (pause now and go get it, because you'll want it throughout this book!).

- Print the worksheets out so you can write directly on them.

- Use the stories in this book as an example of how to implement the Values First Framework in your life.

- Take action—do the worksheets and make the changes needed in your life to live with your Values First.

- Join the Values First community and get extra support at thecatchgroup.com/valuesfirst.

In this book I'll tell you stories about my missteps, my learnings, and some of my proudest moments while referencing the stages in my career. I've worked as a consultant, had jobs in corporate Fortune 50 companies, worked in non-profit, and built my own company. I've held multiple roles, from having my first job as a consultant fresh out of graduate school to being a first-time manager; to holding a job in the C-suite as the chief learning officer and later, founding a company.

I've been an individual contributor (didn't have a team or someone who reported to me), had one direct report, led small teams, and also led big teams. I've managed people who have managed other people. I've been in many different roles, had promotions, lateral transitions, and have switched companies throughout my career. I've had many managers, including some that I couldn't stand and some that still motivate me to grow and learn today, even though I don't work for them anymore.

As I share with you my many lessons learned, I'll recount stories from my own experience to the best of my recollection. Consider this a career memoir with actionable tools. I've changed the names of some individuals and all companies to give them confidentiality. I'll use the below timeline to reference my career:

- Early career—first job consulting, individual contributor/ manager at Fortune 50 company

- Early mid-career—executive, leading leaders at Fortune 50 company

- Mid-career—senior executive, leading teams at Fortune 50 company, C-suite position in smaller organization

- Late mid-career—entrepreneur and executive coach

My goal is to bring more diversity and authenticity to the workplace. I want to see more authenticity from those in manager positions, senior leaders, and C-suite leaders. That's the mission of my company, The Catch Group: to accelerate the careers of women into more leadership positions and to get more diversity and authenticity in the top jobs at organizations. After being in corporate America as an executive in Fortune 50 companies and in the C-suite myself, I left my big job to pursue what mattered most to me.

What mattered most? My values of growth, development, and advocacy to build a company that focuses on accelerating the careers of women. Every day I get to coach high-achieving women individually or through group coaching.

The only way to make change and lead with your values is to do the work. The good news is, I've made it easy for you in this book, outlining steps you can take and helping you through the full Values First Framework process. Plus, I have support on my website including a workbook, weekly tips, and my podcast, *You Belong in the C-Suite.* Get the help you need at www.thecatchgroup.com/valuesfirst.

I hope this book helps you understand a perspective different than your own. This is my perspective. And let me tell you, as an introvert, it is both freeing to get this down on paper and also extremely terrifying that it is now out in the world. If you are feeling stuck or scared, know that I'm right here with you, pushing through and sharing my wisdom.

Enjoy the process, dig in, and happy action-taking.

Ready? Where do you start? Well, it's called Values First for a reason. Let's start there.

Values First

Values First

Dig into what matters
most to you, and set the
foundation of your core
values. You'll also get clarity
on what living those values
looks like uniquely to you.

Values First Framework *from The Catch Group*

Setting the Foundation

THERE ARE TIMES IN YOUR LIFE WHEN YOUR VALUES ARE apparent—so ingrained in you that you don't have to think; you just do. Those values come to us through trial and error, practice, and tradition. In this section, you will get clarity on your values to set the foundation of your values-first life.

Growing up, each Christmas our family of six would pile into our silver Toyota minivan with maroon cloth interior and drive a few hours to east Texas to cut down our tree. Yes, that's totally a thing. Think red barn, hot cider, tractor pulling a trailer with seats made from hay to sit on as the tractor drops you off in the middle of a field of trees. You can bring your own saw or borrow one of theirs (usually rusted and super dull, but those make for better memories). Then the search for the perfect tree would begin.

It had to be tall enough, round enough, and not have too many bare spots in the branches. If it did have bare spots, could it be turned around to hide its imperfections when on display? The trunk had to be mostly straight.

As a kid, my siblings and I coveted the role of the tree finder. You wanted to be the person that found the one; there's pride in that (I picked this year's tree!). We would get the final okay from my mom, who was the actual decider of the tree we ultimately picked. When you finally found "the one," you took the requisite family picture in front of it, while it was still rooted in the ground. Then (and only then) would my dad get the saw and gloves ready (if he remembered them), squat down, and start sawing down the tree.

My mom would stand up, pushing on the tree, helping with a little force to get it to fall. Then, we would take another picture of my dad with the tree, as if he were showing off a huge fish that he just caught, big enough to win the county fair. He'd carry the tree to the path where the tractor would come by and pick us back up and go to the barn, for the tree to get shaken (to take off all of the loose needles) and bailed (put in a plastic netted wrapping to minimize its size so you could easily put it on the top of your car). They'd measure it and give you the ticket to bring to the woman at the front where you could only pay in cash or with a check.

We'd hang out for a while and then, for some reason we'd ALWAYS, and I mean ALWAYS, stop at Sonic on the way home to eat. We'd get tater tots and the peppermint candy. It was amazing. We didn't eat out a lot, so it was a special treat. Every. Single. Year.

When we got home, we'd take the tree off the car, and my dad would get ready to put it in the tree stand. But before he did that, he'd saw off the bottom of the tree to make it even and also to keep it as a keepsake. My parents kept the sawed-off logs from each tree every year. They displayed them as decorations in a woodpile near the fireplace. It was a memento of that moment. You could look back, and some years it was a thinner trunk, sometimes a thicker one. Over the years, we had more and more tree trunks as our family got older. Every year, we went to the tree farm. It was our family tradition.

When my siblings and I became adults, some of us lived in the same city near each other.

My sister asked me one year, "Want to go get a Christmas tree at a farm?"

"Yes!" I replied, reminiscing of our trips as children.

So, that's what we did; we found a new farm in east Texas. This one was only about an hour away. At the time, I was newly married to my husband, Brian, and my sister had two daughters. We started the tradition again, with Christmas carols playing in the car on the way there and back. We even ate at Sonic on the way home.

One year, it was harder. We had our son by then, still an infant hanging out in his Baby Bjorn strapped to my chest. This trip was comprised of more whining, more complaining from the kids—and eventually everyone—plus we had the baby on top of it. It seemed like a slog, to be honest. No one seemed super happy like the years before, but we went, we did it, darn it—we got our Christmas trees and ate at Sonic on the way home. As we were on the way back, we debriefed the ordeal. Was it worth it? With all the kids, all the driving? Weekends were precious time away from my long commute. I relished those non-driving days. Next year, should we just not do this and get a tree at a lot, or even consider a FAKE tree (blasphemy)?

A few months later, in February, my sister sent me a text. My niece, around nine at the time, had drawn her a picture for Valentine's Day while at school. At the top of the page was "Love is…" printed with a space to draw a picture below. In the picture, she drew all of us at the tree farm. She drew out our whole family. Her picture displayed the love and gratitude she had for our tradition. Even though she wasn't a happy camper on the trip (and didn't eat her lunch, said she'd rather be home, and whined like all of us that day), it had meant something to her. It was stability. It was nostalgia. It was important. It meant love to her.

Reflecting back, this family tradition of getting our tree is a representation of my value of family. Prioritizing the time to keep the tradition alive. Prioritizing the quality time. Prioritizing what matters most.

What matters most to you?

When Your Values Aren't Easily Identified

Sometimes your values aren't so easily identified. Sometimes values show up as a lacking, a longing, or a dissatisfaction. But in that discomfort, you can find clarity.

I was in my mid-career, and I felt lost, lonely, and unhappy. I knew that I was making a difference with my team, and that our work mattered. I dreaded making the commute, and sometimes sat a little longer than I should in my car before walking into the office. I'd finish listening to the true crime podcast or listen to another few minutes of an audiobook before gathering my things and walking from the parking lot into the glass office building.

I couldn't figure it out. Why was I unhappy at this amazing company? Especially after so long? I had been an executive there for years, with a bonus plan to match. I'd gotten to work from home several times a week. I was working with amazing internal clients on the business, making a big impact. I was active in our employee resource groups and had deep relationships that I'd built over years.

I started looking for another opportunity within the same company, convinced I just needed to work on something new, to make a different kind of impact. I'd been there for so long; I'd gotten to do so much.

I started reaching out to my mentors within the company. I scheduled time with a previous manager, who had championed my career in spaces that I wasn't yet in. I told him about what wasn't going well and asked for his advice. I was hoping for an honest conversation, feedback, his perspective, and a way forward.

We sat in a talk room designated in the open-office environment for meetings or conversations that you didn't have out in the open. I inquired about his team, what it looked like, and if there were any opportunities upcoming. He told me the timing wasn't right and specific roles wouldn't come open any time soon. That was fair.

He said, "Careers at the company are like a wave. Sometimes, you have a long wave, sometimes you have a short one. And you need to know when the ride on your wave is over."

Was he telling me that my ride was over? Was he saying his ride was over? I've never surfed before; is there more meaning in this than I was giving it? In that small room with the sliding glass door, I realized that maybe he really wasn't a sponsor for me anymore. What I had wanted—an honest conversation—wasn't what I got; or was it? I walked out of that room feeling even more alone.

Well, if my ride was over, what was it like on another wave? Whether that was his intended message or not, after that day, I started looking for roles externally. I started reaching out to people who had left the company a few years before. What was it like? Were they happy? Did they regret it?

I lined up a breakfast meeting with Mark, a full-hearted straight talker who could tell a story and make you cry with laughter, who also happened to bake the best cupcakes I've ever eaten (that buttercream icing…so good). He'd left for a vice president position the year before. We met at a small bistro close to the office. It was a frequent breakfast meeting spot, a place that you'd almost always run into someone you knew. Sitting at our booth, Mark could tell that I was not myself. In his real, candid way, he asked, "What's really going on?"

I looked around to make sure there wasn't anyone in earshot and said, "I'm not happy. I don't know what I should be doing next. I've given so much to this company, and don't feel like I have any sponsors left here," I blurted out.

He said, "There is something deeper going on here. What is it? As soon as you can name it, then you can start to work through it." Yes, there was something else, but what was it? It wasn't only the external circumstances around me. It was something coming up from somewhere deeper, internally.

The concept of naming something to then work through comes from Siegel and Bryson's book, *The Whole-Brain Child: 12 Proven Strategies to Nurture Your Child's Developing Mind.* The strategy called "Name It to Tame It" focuses on corralling the raging right-brain behavior through left-brain storytelling, appealing to the left brain's reasoning to calm emotional storms and bodily tension.[1] If you can label it, then you can start to work through the tension.

I knew I needed to find it and name it.

Naming Your Values

MY BREAKFAST WITH MARK WAS CAREER DEFINING AND encouraged me to dig deeper into what was bothering me; to name it. I took his advice and dug into it all. I started on a journey to define my foundation.

The unfulfillment had drained me and led me to question myself and my competence. *If I wasn't happy here, there must be something wrong with me, I thought.* I needed to start at the foundation. I needed to be grounded. My values are the foundation where everything I chose to build should rest upon, should fit. My foundation needed to be solid.

Over the years, I'd done multiple exercises to identify my values, my core beliefs, and motivations. I like guided exercises like this because if you just asked me to write what my values were, I'd probably write a lot of generic things like "honesty and integrity." My values wouldn't be much different than a stranger's sitting next to me. It is easy to not dig very deep or do the work because sometimes it isn't fun peeling back the onion, especially when you aren't in a happy place. And I wasn't.

I needed a place to start, a language to use—something to describe my melancholy and unfulfillment. The concept of values seemed like a way to use descriptors to put names to the things

I needed or thought were missing. Through my own experience and that of the countless leaders I'd worked with, I built the Values First Framework.

What exactly is a value? As defined, core values are principles or beliefs that a person or organization views as being of central importance.[2] What a big question—what is of central importance to you?

To support you in uncovering this big question, I created a guided worksheet. If you haven't downloaded it yet, go to thecatchgroup.com/valuesfirst to download your Values First workbook. The Values First Framework starts with—you've guessed it—identifying your values. Go to your workbook to dig into what matters most to you using the **Values Worksheet.**

This exercise has three parts to it:

1. Use reflection questions to help gain clarity on your values.

2. Identify the core values that resonate most with you.

3. Identify your secondary values.

It's a profoundly life-changing exercise and the core of living your life with your values first, so be sure to take time to do all three parts. It should take about thirty minutes. You've got this! Let's get started.

First, to get clarity on your values, start by answering a few reflection prompts:

- Think about a time that you were at your best; what were you doing?

- Think about a time that you were really uncomfortable, a time something didn't sit right in your gut. What was that like? How did you feel?

When I did this for myself, I wrote about being my best when I was building the capability of others—one leader at a time. Having them see the insight for themselves and begin to make progress on it filled me with a sense of purpose. I wrote about getting better as a coach, about building my own capability, and figuring out exactly which question to ask that would lead to a path of self-discovery for the person I was coaching.

I wrote about getting to know the business more through these leaders and connecting the dots. I wrote about seeing them work through a problem or having the confidence to ask for a job that they wanted or a raise that they deserved. I wrote about hearing them say no and making the right decisions for themselves and their families. That felt amazing—spending time looking at and defining when I was at my best.

The second prompt involves looking at the opposing side: when I wasn't at my best. It seems a bit counterintuitive to look at a time that wasn't so great to figure out what you value. Why should I want to think about a time that wasn't that great?

Susan David describes in her book, *Emotional Agility*, that our emotions are a sign of our values—what really matters to us.[3] On Brené Brown's podcast, *Dare to Lead*, Susan described how feelings of anger often come up in situations where we feel rooted in something that we care about. Anger is the sign that a value might not be being met. By reflecting on a negative situation, you may uncover a connection to a value that is deeply important to you.[4] In this discomfort, I found clarity.

For the second question, I wrote about being unsettled in my role because I didn't have a next path for myself. It was an uncomfortable time in which I wasn't being challenged, and I didn't see a way forward for me at the organization. I had accomplished what I wanted in the role and if I stayed, then would I be learning anything? It would likely be more of the same.

The next part of the exercise is to identify core values that resonate with you based on the answers to the two questions. Within the worksheet, there is a list of words for you to start from. Use the themes or feelings from the prompts to pick up to seven words that represent your values. There isn't a magic number here, but I've found when working with my clients that choosing more than seven values begins to become overwhelming. Be choosy: which values are most important to you?

Don't worry if you can't find the perfect word. Feel free to add in words to describe your values. Sometimes the easiest thing to do is to cross out the ones that don't resonate first. I realized that by picking out feelings or words from the writing prompts, I could identify my descriptors more easily. For instance, when I wrote about when I was at my best, I was coaching others. Out of the list, I identified development. I loved *developing* teams and leaders.

When I wrote about not learning anything new in my role in the second prompt, I realized that I really need to be developed and challenged in a role. I identified growth as another value that resonated with me. I defined this as my own *growth*. If I wasn't learning, I wasn't growing.

I realized that something is a value if you feel completely uncomfortable or gut-wrenched if you aren't living what you truly believe. That was how I was feeling. I was sitting in something that was, at my core, not right. It didn't sit well with me, and I needed to put a label to it.

Because, as Mark suggested, if you can name it, label it, and understand where it is coming from, you can stop giving it power and, ultimately, fix it. You can fix it in your environment or change your environment.

Through this work, I identified my six core values:

- Family

- Growth

- Development

- Achievement

- Advocacy

- Balance

At the core, this is what motivates me. Those values are my foundation. When I have that great day, it is because I'm plugged into one or more of them. If those values aren't met, I'm miserable and my husband and kids are most likely miserable as well (because I can't stop talking about it—lucky them), until I name it and get my power back. When a value isn't being met either at home or at work (it doesn't have to be met in both places), then I feel stuck. I feel like, *Huh, did I pick the right thing to do with my life? What do I want to be when I grow up (even though I'm mid-career)? Did I make a wrong decision?* Things feel uneasy.

You've now answered the prompts and have chosen your core values. Lastly, identify secondary values. Secondary values are other values that are similar to your core values, or values that came close to being in your top seven but didn't make the cut. In time, you'll revisit your values, and sometimes secondary values can rise to core values as you evolve or become more in tune with what matters to you.

I was once asked, "Can values be bad? What if someone chooses a value that intentionally or unintentionally harms others?" For instance, picking a value of power. Although power has been misused repeatedly—both systemically and individually—inherently, power isn't bad. It is how power is used that can be harmful to others. For the record, any values or behaviors that cause harm to others or uphold patriarchal, misogynistic, or racist values shouldn't be utilized within this framework (or ever). I hope that you not only choose values that don't cause harm, but that they repair and advocate for others with the privilege you hold.

Look at your values list. How does that feel? Does anything need adjusting? Do you already feel more aligned simply by naming them?

Knowing your values and getting clarity on what you value are ways to ground yourself in what is authentically you. It is a foundation. Being rooted in your values serves as a guide to being authentically you.

Clarity Through Values

HAVING A CLEAR UNDERSTANDING OF MY VALUES HAS helped me in many facets of my life and career. The biggest piece of feedback that I've gotten over my lifetime is to "smile more." Maybe that isn't advice, but more of a direct order. I get this directive by people I know sometimes, but mostly by complete strangers (usually men).

"Hey, smile!" they'd say.

"Hey, don't look so serious!" they'd jokingly demand.

"Hey, what's wrong? You should smile more," they'd suggest.

Gaining clarity in my values has helped me understand what feedback to act on and which feedback to leave alone. Over time, I've gotten better at knowing the difference.

In my early career, I worked for a company that had a strategic alliance with a research group from a university. A few times a year, the CEO would bring the university team into the office to share insights to guide our business priorities or products. It was a coveted meeting to be a part of (in my early career), and a few months into my role, I was invited. I was more than excited to be there. I had on a cream-pressed suit with a flowy shirt with just the right amount of yellow in it. As I look back at these instances, I recall not only how I was feeling but what I was wearing, too (weird?).

I was uber-prepared, had read the pre-reads, and I was excited to soak it all in. During the presentation, I anticipated hearing about actionable things that we could do to impact our product line. As they presented, there was a ton of great research, but I couldn't see how it translated into direct impact to our business. Was I missing something?

After the presentation was finished, the CEO asked everyone in the room to go around and give our feedback. I was repeating, *Don't pick me first, don't pick me first, don't pick me first,* in my mind as I averted my eyes downward, avoiding eye contact with him. He scanned the room, and of course, invited me to go first. I had never been in a meeting like this before, at this new job, in my cream suit. I felt sweaty. I didn't know what to say. I wasn't ready.

With a death grip on my pen, I said, "I'm still thinking through it, can I not go first?" I wish I could say that I said something different, but that's what came out of my mouth.

"No, if you don't have anything to say, then I'm not sure why you are here," said the CEO. My stomach dropped, and I looked down. My overachieving, people-pleasing, all A's since elementary school heart broke into pieces.

Just like that, I was dismissed, and that was that. I was shut out of the conversation. My manager, who was also in the meeting, gave me a look. I was expecting it to be a "Wow, he's a jerk" look, but instead it was a "Why didn't you have an answer?" look.

Cue the longest silence known to humankind. Time stood still. I may have aged a year in that sprawling quiet.

My manager ended the awkwardness with, "I'll go. It's great, but I'm having a hard time seeing how the research fits into practical application of our products and services."

"Right," agreed the CEO, "It is interesting, but where is the takeaway here?"

I'd missed an opportunity. My gut was right. I didn't say anything because I thought I wasn't ready.

There's a lot to unpack there: thoughts like, *Will I say the right thing? Am I smart enough to be in this room? Am I confident that my voice matters?* In hindsight, I could have asked a question, or given my initial feedback (which I did have). Imposter syndrome stuck to my legs in my cream suit pants like sweat on a hot day. I didn't even have a chance to be mansplained to because I didn't give my opinion.

Could he have been nicer? Sure, but he wasn't that kind of leader. I already knew that. I didn't trust my own instinct because I was afraid that my answer was wrong or that my opinion wouldn't be the right one. I didn't trust my thoughts enough to speak them.

A decade later in my career, I was in a director position itching to do something new after being in my role for a few years. My second-level manager called me one day to talk about a new role. It was an individual contributor role, doing organizational interventions and capability-building for departments at headquarters. The warning bells in my mind went off. It didn't feel like the right fit for me: less scale and impact, fewer employees to benefit from the work I was doing, no direct reports. That all equaled smaller to me, a step back.

My manager wanted me to get out of my comfort zone of being in a support function, to get out from behind the research and the data. He pushed me to get more client-facing experience beyond what I was already doing in human resources. He wanted me to be in front of the room, in the room, and to have a seat at the literal table. The introvert in me did not want to be the center of attention. I specifically sought out seats in the back of the room, against the wall, out of the way.

My manager, Jeff, was a front-of-the-room kind of person, telling stories and building capability, training on leadership skills.

I wasn't a trainer; I wasn't a facilitator. That stuff terrified me. But he said I would be able to build my toolset and make a difference with the relationships and organizational interventions.

He mentioned I'd get to do more executive coaching. *Well, why didn't he lead with that?* That was my favorite thing to do. Executive coaching is one-on-one. You get to know the strengths and opportunity areas of an individual based on multiple data points, and then get to coach them through their own self-discovery to get better. More opportunities for executive coaching sealed the deal for me.

My first day in the job was an offsite leadership team meeting in Napa, California. What a way to start out a new job—wine and sun! After a night in the hotel, Jeff and I arrived early to the meeting room to get the lay of the land. There were three long tables put together to form a U-shape. Since there was no seat "in the back," I didn't know where I should sit. I picked a spot near the outer end of the parallel sides of the U, so I could see everyone and take it all in.

Within a few minutes, everyone started trickling in. I said good morning to the few people I knew and stayed in my seat. The room was filled with vice presidents and the department leader who was in the C-suite. I was there to facilitate part of their team development activity that afternoon, but that got me a ticket to the whole meeting.

I had prepped for hours, poring over their data to ensure that I made the right connections. The exercise showed the variety of things that motivated them. There were people highly motivated by recognition, some that were motivated by giving back to the community, and others that were motivated by working hard and playing harder.

During the meeting, I listened; I soaked it all in. Jeff kicked off our session, and I facilitated my section at the end of the first day. They laughed when they were supposed to laugh and asked questions. I had done my part at the front of the room. I could finally stop rehearsing what I was going to say in my head.

That night, we had a dinner at a winery. That is an understatement. As you entered the winery, you were brought down to a cave, dimly lit with table rounds decorated with beautiful floral arrangements—as if we had walked into a fancy-schmancy wedding reception, not a work function. There were even pashmina wraps on the back of each chair in case you got a chill (I still have mine).

Exhausted from the day, I was hoping not to have to make small talk with someone I didn't know at dinner. I ended up being seated at a table next to Jeff, thank goodness, and a vice president. The VP was one of those people that made you feel like he was paying attention. He wasn't one of those guys who's too busy for you or has something else on his mind when he's talking to you. He made you feel seen. He asked me about my family, and I talked about my son, who was an infant at the time. He told me about his daughter, and about traveling too much sometimes in his job. Our table had great conversations, laughed, and told stories.

About midway through dinner, he asked me, "Where has this person been? You barely said anything all day in the meeting."

I smiled shyly, "I like to get my bearings and listen to learn; besides, I didn't even know what they were talking about most of the time."

He said, "Sometimes, an outside perspective is exactly what we need. You were picked for the role because you are valued. If you have a question, ask it; if you have a suggestion, say it. We want to hear from you."

I needed to lean into my value of growth and be okay with being uncomfortable not knowing everything. This idea of what I'm supposed to do, or who I'm supposed to be has gotten in my way over the course of my career. As an executive coach, I'm never nervous in any of my conversations with my clients. In my job, I would coach key leaders—the company's top talent, identified based on their performance and their stretch to bigger roles in the future. They'd get an executive coach to accelerate their development even faster. The organization was investing in them.

When these leaders found out that they were selected to be in a leadership program with a coach, overwhelmingly, most of them thought it was because they did something wrong. Quite the opposite. They were top talent that the organization wanted to invest in. The organization wanted them to accelerate their progression in the company, and they were sending them to a leadership program to do that. The company was effectively saying, "Hey leader, we want to accelerate your growth because you are awesome!" Those leaders usually had no idea they were key talent (some companies don't share that information because it can change from year to year). But the leaders should feel it. They should feel like they are being invested in.

So here I am literally coaching leaders on the same stuff— women who are VPs at Fortune 50 companies and who hold C-suite titles at Fortune 500 companies—telling them, "You are valued. You are amazing. You are getting called out because you did some really great stuff, and we want you to do some more really great stuff, so we are investing in you."

"Believe it," I tell them. "You are amazing. Believe it and keep going. Even when it is uncomfortable."

The irony that I need this coaching, too, is not lost on me. Trust yourself. I say it to the executives I coach, and it is a reminder for myself.

Knowing your values can bring you clarity in many situations. It can serve as a filter of what feedback to act on and what feedback to leave alone.

In my mid-career, I had been in a job for about six months; it was the end of our fiscal year, and I received feedback on my performance through a 360-degree feedback survey. In a 360 survey, you get holistic feedback from multiple stakeholders: a 360-degree view of your performance. You rate yourself, your manager rates you, your peers rate you, your direct report rates you, and sometimes your clients can rate you and provide feedback as well. When you take part in 360 feedback process, it takes several weeks for your stakeholders to give feedback in the system, and then you get the report weeks later.

I love this feedback because it is fuel for my growth and development values. I always want to get better. I like constructive feedback. Negative feedback without examples drives me bananas because it limits the action I can take to improve without further context. But without examples, or even if feedback is given poorly, it is still a data point to be considered for growth and development.

I wrote my dissertation on 360 feedback. I have used it for coaching clients for over ten years and managed big 360 processes in companies. I've seen hundreds, if not thousands, of 360 reports in my career.

After receiving their report, the first thing that people usually do is go to the open-ended comments. This is the part that has verbatim comments from the people that rated you. Usually, the answers are masked for their confidentiality, so you don't know who said what (unless they describe a situation that identifies them). The questions are usually, "What are Laura's strengths? What can Laura do to become even more successful in her role? Or what is holding Laura back?" Manager comments are usually identified so you can have a deeper conversation with your manager, who should be supporting your development.

When I received my report, I jumped into the open-ended comments for "opportunity areas." I wanted to see what I needed to do to become better.

After reading through the comments, a familiar theme emerged (I had gotten 360 reports previously). "Laura needs to take up more space" and "She doesn't have gravitas." It isn't new for women to get feedback like this, and it surely wasn't the first time I had gotten this feedback.

As a leader, you can work on the things that are your opportunity areas. But guess what: however much work you put into them, they will most likely never magically turn into strengths. I knew that I was not going to be able to change my personality into being an extrovert. Nor did I want to. That isn't me. That's not authentically who I am.

The feedback on taking up more space and having gravitas didn't feel authentic for me to respond to or take action on. How do I take up more space? Like at a table? What is gravitas anyway? I asked a few people what they thought it meant, and I got definitions like "charisma" or "gregariousness" and "authoritativeness." I really wanted to know about this word, so I looked it up. It means high seriousness.

If there was a word that *did* describe me, it was gravitas. I'd been told my whole life to lighten up and not be too serious. But in this context, gravitas didn't make sense. The feedback on my limited gravitas seemed very masculine to me. My first interpretation was, Be more like a man? More research on this gravitas word taught me that among the Romans, gravitas was "thought to be essential to the character and functions of any adult male in authority."[5]

It was real feedback, but should I prioritize my time on it? Is it something that I should focus on? Am I getting results? Am I driving the strategy forward? Am I building relationships in a meaningful way? Am I developing my team? Am I meeting or beating my goals?

Instead of taking up space, I reframed it as holding space for myself. Do I need to hold my space at the table, stretch out, have my coffee and my sparkling water, with my notebook and my bag? As an introvert, I generally don't draw attention to myself. Now when I am at the table, I have become very cognizant of not minimizing myself or my physical presence. I'm holding that space for me and being my authentic self. And that, I will do with gravitas.

In my career, I've been invited into spaces where I don't feel like I belong. It is uncomfortable and I question why I am there. My whole life, I've gotten the feedback to speak up. By listening to the feedback I get and filtering it through what matters most to me—my values—I can figure out what feedback to take and what feedback to leave.

I use my values of growth and development to steer towards my authentic self and away from listening to every piece of feedback given (because sometimes people are jerks or may be having a bad day). That's why it is so important to have clarity when you are living your values.

So far you have named your values and gotten clarity on them. Now let's help you realize when you are living them.

Your Ideal State

LET'S DEFINE WHAT LIVING YOUR VALUES MEANS TO YOU at this time in your life. Go to your Values First workbook to the **I'm Living My Values When Worksheet.** For each of your core values, list a few specific ways that you know when you'll be successful.

- What does success mean when you are living out that value?

- What does it tangibly look like?

- List feelings and actions.

My example is below.

I know I'm successful in meeting my value of **Family** when

- I eat dinner with the family four nights a week.

- I have quality time with each family member individually (both kiddos and hubby) in a given week.

- I honor the commitment I've made to the kids' schedules within my workday schedule (flex hours), and I am working from home three-plus days a week.

I know I'm successful in meeting my value of **Achievement** when

- I meet my weekly writing goal.

- I have a feeling of accomplishment toward planned tasks.

I know I'm successful in meeting my value of **Development** when

- I coach leaders.

- I give feedback to others with examples.

I know I'm successful in meeting my value of **Growth** when

- I listen to business podcasts and/or read a business or non-fiction book.

- I spend time each week intentionally growing or nurturing my network.

- I get out of my comfort zone and feel uncomfortable.

I know I'm successful in meeting my value of **Advocacy** when

- I donate to organizations that are aligned with my values.

- I educate myself on how to become a better ally.

- I have difficult conversations with people in my life (and not with strangers on the internet).

I know I'm successful in meeting my value of **Balance** when

- I go to bed by 10:30 p.m. at least four nights a week (this is hardest for me).

- I work out more days in a week than I don't.

- I have some alone time.

- I feel that I've been able to set my pace for the week.

- I allocate downtime in my week for reading fiction.

It may be hard to come up with actions or feelings for each of your values. You don't have to commit to all of them. This is just a list. It can give you a picture of what it could look like in the future—what living or feeling your values in your everyday life could be.

Values Vision Boards

If you're more of a visual person or you want to have fun filling out this worksheet, you can create a vision board to express what living your values looks like. In a leadership development program I attended many years ago, I built a vision board. A vision board can be a physical poster board, or it can be digital. I built mine in PowerPoint and Google images. A vision board is a reflective exercise for who you are and who you aspire to be in the future.

The idea is that by visualizing your future desires, you can focus on what it will take to manifest those desires.

After taking a step back from my vision board, I realized that I had visualized my values within the board. For my value of family, I had put in a picture of our family after we had finished a fundraising walk for heart health. For my values of growth and development, I had chosen words to put on the vision board that represented coaching, and also one of my favorite questions— what is the problem to solve? For my value of balance, I put in a picture of an indoor rowing machine, because that's where I get my balance and stress relief—through my workouts. And for my value of advocacy, I put in words and pictures that depicted equity and active listening.

Go to the workbook to build your own **Values Vision Board.** Build a physical representation of your values, of who you are, and what is important to you.

You can use your values vision board in a number of ways.

- Take it to an interview to describe your leadership style and what's important to you.

- Use it in one-on-ones with new people on your team.

- Hang it in your office space as a visual reminder of what's important.

After reading this book, my writing coach and her family were inspired by this exercise and built a box for their family's phones. Her sister and nieces put their phones in it at a certain time of day because one of their collective values is being present. They've decorated the box with reminders of the things that matter to them more than their phones—the values important to their family.

Sometimes it isn't enough to see your values in front of you to ground yourself. Sometimes you need an outside point of view to remind you when you were at your best and living your values. I have a hard time tooting my own horn. I mostly attribute this to my introversion and to being a collaborator at heart. Singing the praises of others comes much more naturally, and it feels awkward to do it for myself. Selfish somehow.

Sally Helgesen and Marshall Goldsmith write about this in *How Women Rise.* They outline twelve behaviors holding women back, the first being Reluctance to Claim Your Achievements.[6] The reason behind this behavior is that women don't want to be that person.

You know, *that person* who has the roar of a lion but does the work of a mediocre cat? (I'm a dog person, sorry).

By doing good work and demonstrating their results, women think *the work will speak for itself.* All too often, though, good work goes unnoticed in the fast-paced cultures amongst others in corporate life.

You should talk about yourself or write about yourself—resume writing, for instance. The hardest part of writing about myself on my resume or a profile summary for LinkedIn is always that overview paragraph. Sometimes it comes out too general, or sometimes it comes out too casual. Example: Laura is a strategic business leader with proven business results. I've just described every person on LinkedIn.

After years of being in human resources, I can write a goal and an outcome like nobody's business. I can tell you about business results like there is no tomorrow. What I can't do as well is talk about myself without either sounding like a robot or pouring my heart out. So, now I use a different strategy. I use words from others—words about me, from other people.

Encouragement File

I heard a suggestion in a leadership class to keep an "encouragement" file in an email folder. The strategy is to file all the positive emails you receive from mentors, managers, direct reports, vendors, etc., in one place so that when you are feeling discouraged or unmotivated (or just having a hard day), you can look in that file and see the impact you have made and are making on others.

It reminds you of when you were living your values, and can bring you out of your slump. Comments from previous performance reviews and 360 reviews are also great places to grab words from others about you. There are open-ended comments that are treasure troves of great sound bites about leadership strengths. I save those data points so I can use them later for motivation.

The last time I updated my resume when I was in the job market, I used those emails and those words of others to build out my summary paragraph at the top of the page. Immediately, I saw that it was more authentically written, and more specifically calling out my values in a way I never could have. At the very least, it was a great place to start.

Go to the **Values in Action Worksheet** in your workbook. What are some of the words that others say about you?

Here are a few ideas of where to find them:

- Your performance appraisal

- A thank you note from a client

- An email from a coworker

- Feedback from an interview

- A 360-degree appraisal

- Recommendations from LinkedIn

Those words and descriptions about you, from people you trust, are examples of your values in action. Look at those the next time you need a pick-me-up.

In this section, you have learned the importance of putting your values first, named your values, gotten clarity on what they are, and created a comprehensive list of how you know you are living your values. Congrats, you now have the foundation of living your values-first life.

Now, let's do an audit to see how these values are and are not already showing up for you.

Audit Time

Audit Time

Review your time to see
where your values do and
don't show up in your life,
and learn how to use your
values to make difficult
decisions at home and work.

Values First Framework *from The Catch Group*

Living Your Values

IT ALWAYS SEEMS LIKE THE SIMPLEST THINGS ARE THE hardest to do consistently. Drink water, get a full night's sleep, eat healthy, move your body. We know these things are the right things to do, but we often don't do them. Similarly, knowing your values and living them are different things.

In this section, you will audit how you are living your values in your everyday life. You'll identify what gaps exist and which values are most important to prioritize.

There's always another bonus or long-term reasoning keeping you in place at your job. The system is designed that way, to retain you. Turnover costs money.

Big decisions—like staying at a company or leaving—can feel so heavy and so all-or-nothing. It's because you've worked hard for it all: the title, the tenure, the opportunity to solve the complexities of the organization. You've put in the time and energy to lead bigger teams, to take the more prestigious accounts. If you move on to something else, will it be better than your current job or employer?

If you've felt unfulfilled at work, I'd suggest that you don't have it as good as it could be. The first thing to do is to name it. What is the tension you are feeling? What value is misaligned for you?

For me, it always came back to my values of growth, development, and achievement. If I wasn't growing, or if I wasn't able to achieve within my authentic leadership style, then I felt misaligned and unhappy. At first, it was a feeling I got after a meeting or two within a month. Then it became more recurrent—until the bad days outnumbered the good days. The reward wasn't worth it anymore, no matter how big the bonus was that was dangling out in front of me, months away.

Others have given me advice in the past that it is always easier to find a job while you have a job. Sometimes that isn't possible. Many organizations have layoffs or reductions of force. I've been laid off before. You don't always get to have control over every decision in your career.

I have never wanted to leave a job because I was running away from something, like a bad boss or a bad situation. That would have felt like giving away my power. I always want to leave for something else, on my own terms. In the times that you don't have another opportunity to run to, there's always something you can run towards.

Don't run from a bad situation.
Run towards your values.

After years in consulting and corporate jobs, I find that now, after practicing my values in my everyday decisions, the bigger decisions come a little easier. I keep consistency in the everyday decisions I make about how I spend my time and how my values show up each week. My values center me every day, so when I need to make a bigger decision, clarity comes sooner.

I still ruminate on the big decisions, think about them, discuss them, do my pros and cons lists. Talk to my mentors and others.

But at the end of the day, it comes back to my values. Are my needs being met? Which ones are and which ones aren't? Once I can name them, then I can describe them and make a plan; take that next step forward to the decision that I already really knew I needed to make. Trust yourself, and the right answer will come. Moving from corporate to my C-suite job was like this for me, and moving from my C-suite job to entrepreneurship came the same way. Many considerations, but one answer.

My husband and I went on a marriage retreat weekend several years into our marriage. In the too-cold conference room of a nearby hotel, with four or five other couples in the room, the deacon was describing our next exercise in the workshop.

"The ladies in the room may not find this next exercise very interesting," he said as he introduced the next concept.

He continued, "We'll be doing a SWOT analysis, which is a common business practice. We'll go through Strengths, Weaknesses, Opportunities, and Threats." Cue a big eye roll from me. Of course, a business term, that's why women would find this so boring. Because women don't like business. Right. I eventually tuned back into what he was saying.

"You will focus on the Strengths, Weakness, Opportunities, and Threats of your marriage, just like you would do in a business context."

It was a great exercise despite the horrible introduction to the concept. In business, we are guided by our long-term strategy and annual goals to get closer to that strategy. Businesses and leaders make short-term and long-term decisions based on the organization's strategy. A good strategy will keep you focused. A good strategy will push away bright, shiny objects that may distract you.

Your values are your strategy. Use your values in your everyday life to remain focused and to center yourself—to ensure you aren't getting distracted by a new thing or opportunity because everyone else is doing it. Use your values for the long-term to make the big decisions. Like a business strategy, review your values often. Stress test them, do they still hold up for you? Use your values as a filter for the everyday stuff and the big stuff. Your values are your guide.

That new volunteer opportunity at work your manager asked you to do? Where does it show up according to your values? Do you have time for it? Does it meet a need? Just because you can do something or are good at it, doesn't mean it is the opportunity for you at this time. You can say no, and you should be saying no to things if they don't align with your strategy or your values (what's important to you).

Use your values as a strategy to make those big decisions, too. Leave that job that makes you feel unfulfilled. Accept that other job offer that is a bigger risk. Leave the bonus on the table because there is more opportunity on the other side.

Make the big decisions to live your values.

Values Check-in

ONE WAY TO MAKE BIG DECISIONS IS TO CHECK IN WITH your values.

Once you've identified your values and defined what living them looks like, you can understand where and how your values show up. Do they show up only on the weekends? Or only once in a blue moon after everything else gets done? You may not have the luxury of setting your own schedule day after day, but how are you spending the time you do have control of? An exercise called the **Values Check-in** has helped my clients pinpoint where their core values play out in their everyday lives.

The **Values Check-in** consists of two questions that examine each of your values.

1. Where does the value show up in my life?

2. How do I feel about it?

For example, two of my values are growth and development, so I would ask myself: where does growth show up in my life?

My professional growth shows up when I'm leading a new project at work. You know those projects that seem overwhelming at first, with a lot of competing deadlines and numerous people to communicate with? I learn the most through critical experiences, and that value shows up at work.

Where does my value of development show up in my life? It shows up in my coaching engagements with women leaders. I love to be able to see the growth in others and help them find insights to solve problems and reach their goals. That's fulfilling for me. A tangible example of how that value shows up in my day-to-day life is through meetings with leaders that I coach.

Now for the second question—how do I feel about it? For the value of growth, I feel great when I have new, challenging projects that I'm working on. It feels not so great if I'm at a point where I don't see that value showing up at work. I feel bored or restless somehow. For the value of development, if I'm spending more of my time coaching leaders, then I'm feeling great about meeting that value.

No judgment on what your answers are. If you don't feel great about a core value, it is an indicator that you have some work to do to live that value; it is a gap that needs to be filled. The goal is to get an understanding of where you are—a values baseline, per se. At the end of this exercise, you should have clarity on where your values do and do not show up in your life and how you feel about it. It shouldn't be a surprise that if you don't see where that value shows up in your life, you may have neutral or negative feelings.

If you can't figure out where a value shows up in your life, you may not be focusing on it right now, or maybe you just lost the opportunity to have it in your life. Have a conversation with a trusted friend or family member. Ask them where they see you living this value. They may have an outside perspective that triggers this for you.

Additional points of reflection can also be helpful to consider.

- What if you have identified where it shows up, and you have neutral or negative feelings about it?

- What could that mean?

- When was the last time you felt connected to this value?

- What is a positive experience when you think of that value?

Review your answers holistically.

- How does the bigger picture feel?

- Is it made up of positive feelings, negative, a mix?

- Is there one value that resonates with you most, for better or worse?

- Are there values at this point that don't resonate with you as much?

- Is it because you are doing well with them right now?

- Are they not a priority for you at this season of life? Or is it not a core value?

Focus on the insights that you take from your reflection.

One time in my mid-career, after my conversation with Mark, I did this exercise for myself. For my values of growth and achievement, I couldn't find a place where they were showing up in my life. And I didn't feel good about it. For development, I was actively developing my team, and I felt good about that.

But that was outweighed by the gap I felt in not living out my values of growth and achievement. By staying in that role, I was compromising my own values.

By compromising my values, I was compromising my (and my family's) happiness, my fulfillment. I was also compromising my value to the world.

What parts of your life are you compromising by not living your values? What are the impacts of that?

Women often compromise their values because society tells them what it means to be successful. That is why it is so important to check in with your values when making big decisions. My client, McKenzie, was a great example of that.

McKenzie was a senior executive in a multi-billion-dollar health and wellness company. Through her career, she had worked at smaller, mid-sized companies. The company she worked for was one of those, until they were acquired and were now part of a bigger corporation. When I started working with McKenzie, she knew she wanted to advance her career, but she wanted to first build a new long-term strategy at her current company.

One of her core values was influence. Upon reflection, when she was living her value of influence, she had a direct connection to the decision-makers of the organization—the CEO and the board. Her value of connection was also important to her, building long-term relationships and providing long-term value to clients. Company culture was also very important to her to meet this value.

She was contacted by a recruiter to join a mid-sized company as a senior executive. In this role, McKenzie would be building a new function, which was a strategic priority for the board and CEO. She knew she would thrive in the culture, which was forged on building relationships, working hard, and celebrating successes—it was part of the organization's DNA. But in the end, she ended up turning down the job, because it was a lateral move and not a promotion. Plus, she still had things she wanted to accomplish in her role at her current company.

McKenzie is a member of my coaching program, and later she identified her values and defined what they meant for her. Then she audited her time. Was she living her values of influence and connection? Reflecting on her calendar, she realized she spent most of her time in cross-functional meetings within her big company. In these meetings, it felt like a struggle to influence with impact.

Even though she had a lot to contribute, she found that she couldn't influence the way she wanted to. She didn't feel like she was able to influence or build relationships. She wasn't living her values at work.

This realization led her to think through what she really wanted to accomplish in this role. It also left her questioning why she turned down the other job offer. Did she really care about the bigger job title? Or was that an external objection she thought she would receive? The story going through her head was that of other people's reactions to her taking a lateral position at a company that was smaller in size. She questioned this external objection because achievement was not one of her core values. Why did that matter to her?

She took the weekend to think through what she really wanted, and how she could fully live her values and contribute the way she wanted to in an organization that she would thrive in. The following week, she called the recruiter back to talk about the position she had previously declined. McKenzie had built a relationship with the recruiting team and had left the option open to talk again in the future if they could find another opportunity. Of course she had, because that's what McKenzie does; she's a connector. They were thrilled that she had reached out and extended her a stronger offer, which she enthusiastically accepted.

Often, we think the best way to be fulfilled is to keep climbing the corporate ladder higher and higher, but sometimes satisfaction comes from the lateral moves or the critical experiences. McKenzie second-guessed her initial thought that success meant a promotion; it really meant getting a new critical experience in her career to live her values of influence and connection.

Alignment with Values

AFTER DOING A CHECK-IN, I WAS ABLE TO PINPOINT THAT the root of my unhappiness in my current position was the lack of achievement and growth in my life. Once I named it, I couldn't ignore it. Those values were flashing at me like a school bus backing up with the red lights flashing (*beep—beep—beep*), every single day that they weren't being met.

As I started to look for another opportunity externally, those values became my guide, my ruler by which to measure other opportunities against, along with a few other things that I knew I wanted. My value of family guided me to want more work-from-home days. And my value of development urged for more breadth beyond the current industry I was in. The value of advocacy pushed me toward the ability to make a bigger impact with my work.

I literally put these criteria in a checklist and mapped out my job search, networking, and other opportunities, like starting my own consultancy. What would fulfill me? How would my values show up in my work? For any job opportunities that came to me, I compared them against my checklist. That checklist reminded me what mattered most.

If the job opportunity didn't check the boxes, then I wouldn't apply for it. Or if I found out new information about the role through the interview process and it went against the checklist, I dropped out of the interview process. For instance, I interviewed with one company multiple times, but realized it wasn't that much different than my current employer and wouldn't give me the growth I wanted, so I dropped out of the interview process.

In my job search, I connected with some trusted colleagues in my network. I saw a position that checked all the criteria—global organization, leading a big team, mission driven. I read the job description of the role and the qualifications. I didn't know much about the organization, but I knew someone who was interviewing with them at the time. I did some research on their website and their social media presence, where I found another job description of the same job.

This job description was more detailed and showcased more qualifications—qualifications that I clearly didn't have. I wasn't a global citizen. I grew up and lived in the United States for my entire life. I had global roles previously but didn't get to travel much because of cutbacks around travel and expenses—and so on and so on, I told myself. And in that moment, I decided not to apply.

In the next several weeks, I met a friend for lunch to catch up on our job searches. She told me about a company that she was working for. It was the same company as the job I didn't apply for. She told me about a job there that she thought I'd be a good fit for. It was the role I didn't apply for, the job I thought was "too big" for me.

I told her point blank, "I'm not qualified for that job."

In return she said, "You can do that job, Laura. Of course you can. Apply for it."

I went home and reviewed the job description again. Now centered in my values, I submitted my resume online.

I put my resume in the box.

Women often have stories running through their heads telling themselves reasons why they can't do something, why they aren't good enough, why someone else is better. The research tells us that women tend to underrepresent their resumes and downplay their skills. They think they must have 100 percent of the qualifications on a job description to even apply.[7]

Self-worth and acceptance aren't linear things. At this point in my career, I had defined what I wanted and needed to live a life that I loved. But life is sneaky; just when you have a breakthrough, you can start to doubt yourself in this spiral of *I'm not worthy or good enough.*

This still happened to me, mid-career. But what happens now is that I can get back to my values. I can shut that shit down. Of course, the doubt creeps in and inaction takes hold. I had convinced myself not to apply. And then, after the pep talk and more information from more credible sources than my limiting beliefs (my friend), I applied.

History has a funny way of repeating itself. My self-doubt repeated itself, first in the early stages of my career—not wanting to apply for one job I didn't think I was qualified for—and then again much later in my mid-career. The outcomes were also repeated. I got that first job in my early career that I almost didn't apply for. I also got the job in my mid-career I almost didn't apply for.

Mantra reminder: put your resume in the freaking box.

Here are a few things you can do when searching for job that aligns with your values.

- Define your criteria aligned with your values—I built mine using an app on my phone.

- Talk to people in your network that are doing the thing that you want to do.

- Find opportunities and companies aligned with your values. If they don't meet the criteria, then that isn't the right place for you.

You've checked in on your values. Now let's take a deeper dive to ensure you are living your values every day.

Values Calendar Review

TO MAKE PROGRESS ON UNDERSTANDING HOW TO MEET your values, you can dig into how you spend your time. To do this, you may need a **Values Calendar Review.**

If you are in the business world, you most likely live by a calendar and some kind of task list to ensure you get all of your work done (and don't forget a colleague's birthday). You manage that through a digital calendar or in a physical planner of some kind. You may be one of those people that hate calendars, and I get that. Some people have a set schedule and don't need a calendar to remind themselves what to do or where to go next. But the rest of us are getting old, and our brains need that written help.

The goal of the **Values Calendar Review** is to understand how you spend your time and align it with your values. If you have a digital or paper calendar, you may only be tracking how you spend your time in meetings during working hours. If I looked at a regular work calendar for a given week, there are empty slots when I am in between meetings. What did I do during those times? Besides eating lunch, I can tell you that I most likely caught up on email or did project work. I might have had a quick conversation about a project. I don't always account for work like that because it isn't project- or meeting-based.

To start, track how you spend your time for a week in the **Values Calendar Review Worksheet** in your workbook. This sounds tedious, and it kind of is. No judgment, just track it. If you binged Netflix on Sunday afternoon, write it down. I find it helpful to write it down in time increments of thirty minutes. Use the notes app on your phone or a notebook to keep a running tally of how you spent your time for a week in real time. Each day, write out a summary of how you spent your time. Ensure that you add in the unaccounted-for hours after work or on the weekend that you don't usually schedule in for work and non-working hours. Put in the details about the appointments for yourself and your family (drop off kid number one at soccer and pick up kid number two from dance, workout, etc.).

At the end of the week, review your time and reflect on the following questions:

1. What surprised you most? In a good way or not-so-good way?

2. What aha moments did you have?

3. What are you going to celebrate?

4. What do you need to recalibrate?

After finishing this exercise, I realized how much time I spent on my phone. I looked at my Screen Time app and reviewed what I was looking at most. I realized that some of my unallotted time was scrolling through different social media apps. I also noticed that I have a consistent weekday routine with the family, and the weekends tend to be more flexible.

The next step in the **Values Calendar Review** is to label your time based on your values. You may not be able to code every entry. For each time entry, review it and see if it reflects one of your values. Don't spend too much time on this; go with your gut.

Here are a few examples from my review of one day.

Activity	Value
Rowing twenty minutes in the morning	Balance
Assortment of project meetings	Not tied to value
Lunch with the kids	Family
Coaching clients	Development
Walk outside for forty-five minutes	Balance
Writing time	Growth
Scrolling on Instagram	Not tied to a value

In a given day, you may not have met all of your values. Throughout the week, some trends have emerged. Different values show up on different days.

For further reflection, go back to your **Values Worksheet.**

- For the values that you identified with feelings of fulfillment, are they reflected more in your week? Those may show up more in your calendar than the ones that you marked with neutral or negative feelings.

- What if you don't see your values represented within your week?

- Were those values that had more neutral or negative feelings associated with them?

Over the course of a month, you want to see a reflection of your values somewhere. You can't prioritize everything. Some values may need to take priority in a given week or month. If it feels unresolved or unsettling in any way to not have your values met—like something is missing—then you can work towards a plan to get those values met.

Many clients do a calendar review and may feel shame or frustration. Give yourself grace. This isn't about judgment; it's about where you are aligned with your values. It gives you a way to prioritize what's important, the right next step to take in living your values. No matter what the results, doing a calendar review is an accomplishment. Go reward yourself.

During this audit, you learned how to make big decisions by checking in with your values, you reviewed your calendar to see how your values are or are not showing up in your life, and you heard firsthand how checking in with your values can transform your personal and professional life. How does that feel? Pretty great, right?

Next, we are going to talk about everyone's favorite word: boundaries.

Life Boundaries

L

Life Boundaries

Set your Values First priorities to create the boundaries you need to truly live the life that you want, and create a system for keeping those boundaries in place.

Values First Framework *from The Catch Group*

Building a Boundary

AROUND HERE, THE NOTION OF BOUNDARIES ISN'T JUST some self-help fluff thrown around at a corporate retreat. In this section, I'm going to give you the tangible tools you need to not only set boundaries, but also keep them through grace and consistency.

I've never considered myself an athlete. I casually played tennis in high school. I didn't take it too seriously (sorry, fellow junior varsity tennis players from my high school days). A car accident that left me with a recurring back injury kept me from working out in my early twenties (or so I told myself). In my late twenties, I tried to run a few times with the *Couch to 5K* program. That led me to do my one and only 5K. I never considered working out an enjoyable hobby.

In my first pregnancy with my son, I ate for four. Potatoes were my biggest craving. I had to have all the carbs. All of them. I gained sixty-seven pounds in that pregnancy; turns out he was only eight and a half pounds of that. Thank God my mother told me to pack my hospital bag with clothing to fit my pregnant body for coming home after the birth.

She told me that she brought pre-pregnancy clothes with her when she had her first kid (my older sister), not realizing what state her body would be in after having a baby. Your post-birth body isn't like a balloon that flattens when the air gets let out.

I ended up having a Cesarian section—not the birth plan, but everyone was healthy. That meant more healing for me as we got to know each other, this new person they let us bring home.

I focused on breastfeeding (which didn't come easily to baby and me) and taking care of myself and my incision. We slept when the baby slept. We supplemented with formula, a decision that was made between my husband and my mother—out of desperation and exhaustion—I napped one day. It was the right decision for us.

I had taken three months off for my maternity leave, and wish I had taken more to be with him. By the time I went back to work, he was sleeping through the night for the most part, but we were all still exhausted. I was returning to a job that I had been at for a while, so it was good coming back to something I knew so well. When I came back, it was familiar but different. My priorities had shifted; I knew that this family was now the most important thing, as I cried on the commute to the office on my first day back.

Preparing to come back to work was also hard because I didn't fit into any of my clothes. My younger sister served as my stylist as we went shopping for work basics and nursing-friendly tops, because I'd be pumping at work. I wore maternity pants well into post-baby life because they fit better than regular work pants.

Going back to pants with zippers or buttons after wearing stretchy, elastic-waisted pants is a new circle of hell. The few pairs of pants that I did wear with the torturous combination of zipper and button, I unbuttoned as soon as I got into my car. It messed with my confidence, but I had a healthy baby, so it was okay, I told myself. Really, I felt like I'd lost myself and my body somewhere along the way.

On my way home from work, I routinely passed a shopping complex with a new storefront. I saw women periodically going in and out of it and realized it was most likely a workout studio. It felt like something I should check out, like it was time to start focusing on losing the baby weight that I hadn't lost yet, eight months post-pregnancy. As you read this, you might be screaming, "Ugh, why is that your motivation, to lose weight?" What started as a motivation to lose weight (fueled, most likely, by the unattainable expectations that a patriarchal society puts on women to bounce back immediately after having a baby) eventually became a way for me to live out my value of balance.

I got the courage to ask my good friend, Hayley, if she would try out this new studio with me. Hayley is notoriously up for a bargain, and there was a sign-up special for half off your first class. The studio taught low impact, high-intensity workouts including spin, indoor rowing, and ballet barre classes. I convinced her we could handle a barre class—a program with ballet moves. I took ballet as a kid; how hard could it really be?

I was already in pain when the instructor mentioned we were only ten minutes in to the sixty-minute class. *What? How can that be? We've been here forever, eternally forever.* During the barre class, I legit thought my legs would burn out and that I wouldn't be able to walk the twenty feet to my car. I kept thinking about how wonderful it would be to make it through the end of the class so Hayley and I could talk about how we were never, ever coming back in one million years. I couldn't wait to talk about the ridiculousness of it all. What were we thinking?!

I somehow got through the class and did walk out of the doors using my own legs. As I got to my car, I remember thinking that this was the last time I was going to be in this building, ever.

Just as I opened my car door, Hayley looked at me and said, "Well, that was horrible. When are we doing it again?"

"Wait, what? You want to go back?" I questioned, wondering if my friend had lost her mind.

"Yes, we are going back," she said with a smile.

"Ugh, fine," I conceded. "I'll try it one more time." Nothing like peer pressure to help you make good life decisions.

Two days later, I could barely walk. My legs BURNED. It hurt to sit down. It hurt to stand up. That made going to the bathroom painful and ridiculous.

But I did not die. So, we went back. We took more barre classes, and then I got the courage to try an indoor rowing class. It was like a spin class, but instead of a room full of stationary bikes, it was full of indoor rowers. I'd never seen a rowing machine before, besides glancing at a dusty old one in one of those big, anonymous gyms that I paid a monthly fee for but never used.

This indoor rower had a tank full of water at the top end of it with a thing that spun around the tank as you rowed. A big *woosh* sound could be heard as you pushed back. As everyone jumped on their rowers and strapped their feet into the foot stretchers, there were woosh sounds at different cadences across the room. Our instructor, Molly, who reliably had a short bob, smile, and the best nineties and early 2000s hip hop music playing, spent the first few minutes teaching us some terminology and told us to start rowing, even if we didn't know what we were doing. I started and felt like an awkward duckling.

"Start in the catch at the front of the machine, where you are almost tucked in a ball but sitting straight up with your arms out, holding onto the handles, your knees into your chest. Hold on, not too tight, with your pinkies slightly off the handles. Now push back, legs straight out, keeping your arms straight, too. Then tip back, pretend your torso is a clock and you are at twelve right now, lean back to the ten position on the clock, then bring your arms into your sternum, right below the band of your sports bra. Then bring your arms back straight out, keep your legs straight, come back up to the two position on the clock, where your arms are now over your knees, and then slide back into the catch. You've just done a stroke," Molly explained as she did the motions with us, like all of those words made sense to my brain. Eventually I got it, though.

Push off with your legs, lean back with your core, bring in your arms. Bring your arms back out, back up with your core, legs back in. Legs-core-arms, arms-core-legs (one stroke), legs-core-arms, arms-core-legs (two strokes)…and there I was rowing. In the class, there were two sets of five rowers facing towards each other. Molly explained that even though we were on individual rowers, we would row together as if we were in the same metaphorical boat.

"So, let's get in sync together. If we don't, then the boat will tip and we'll be in the water," she said. Where was my metaphorical life vest for this?

The thing about water rowers is that you can't outgrow them, so newbies like me or seasoned rowers were in these classes all together at different skill levels. I was the newbie in this class but could see others around me that knew what they were doing. I wanted to get better at this. My value of achievement started seeping through.

Rowing is the same motion over and over. The repetitive nature of it is mind numbingly boring to some. For others, it is peace. Every time I get to the catch, just before you push off each stroke, I get a chance to start over, to burst, to push. That's a magical place, the catch. It is where your power comes from—just before an explosion of energy to keep you going, then a small pause before you do it all again. Getting to the catch is giving yourself another chance to try again, to explode off the platform, with the force of your whole body—your whole self.

My legs burned as I slid backwards on the rail. With the push and pull, back and forth, I found my rhythm. My mind stayed in the present. I was focused. I was out of my own head. For the first time, I felt connected to something that I really liked in a workout. I'd never experienced that before. I'd always equated working out to something negative—as a punishment for eating too much or an excuse to eat more. Rowing felt like it was mine.

Sometimes you plan for a boundary, and sometimes it finds you. Rowing found me through my value of balance.

Without realizing it, I had filled the gap of balance that I needed in my life. I value balance—time for myself, for just me. As I look back, I built it by listening to what I needed at the time—time for myself for a workout class: my value of balance. Then I built a boundary around it.

I started taking multiple rowing classes a week at the studio. With my husband's support or with childcare when he was traveling for work, I prioritized working out at least three times a week. The community there was mostly women, of different ages and different skill levels. I signed up for workout challenges and met new people. We really were a community.

After several months, I had gotten stronger and, more importantly, found something that I loved to do to move my body. I felt more comfortable in my own skin than ever before.

It became a place where I didn't have to be anyone else but me, for me. I didn't have to be mom, or a wife. Just Laura—for forty-five minutes to an hour several days a week. A me I didn't even know was in there.

I learned that I needed to prioritize my value of balance. I made it a priority and built a boundary to keep that time for myself. I needed to give myself space for me, to relieve stress.

In their book *Burnout: The Secret to Unlocking the Stress Cycle*, Emily Nagoski and Amelia Nagoski describe emotion as a tunnel that you have to move through. Dealing with the stressors or the stress isn't enough. You must complete the cycle. Physical movement is one way to do that. Other ways to complete the cycle are through positive social interaction, laughter, affection, a big ol' cry, or through creative expression.[8] What can you do?

If I'm not balanced, something is off. I now include long walks in this category of finding balance and completing the cycle. I think about it as moving my body. Have I moved my body enough? Am I making progress and clearing my head each week? Not surprisingly, the weeks that I don't prioritize it, those weeks I'm more stressed. I'm not as calm; I have a shorter fuse. The weeks that I do prioritize it, I'm a more patient mom. I'm a more fun person. I feel more accomplished because I've kept that promise to myself.

Balance isn't about work-life balance. Balance is ensuring that I've lived a week in balance with what I need. Balance is giving myself time and space for myself, and having a support system that cares about me enough for that space to be prioritized. Not a balance beam, a teeter-totter.

It isn't about staying on or off the balance beam. It is getting the right needs met in a week. Some weeks are higher, some are lower; but overall, if I'm keeping my boundaries, I feel balanced.

I have tried to meditate so many times. And what runs through my mind is: *I am in my head too much to do this effectively. I'm really bad at it. I cannot stop my mind from wandering. I'm not good at this. I'm not the kind of person who can do this. I'm in my head all the time as an introvert. Shouldn't this be easier for me? Or is it because I'm always in my head, it is harder to clear out my thought-filled mind?* One of my "I'm Living My Values When" definitions for balance is to set my own pace.

Rowing is the closest I've ever gotten to that peace and calm that others tell me come from mindfulness. Rowing is my meditation. Rowing is my place to get so many of my values met that it became a symbol for me—so much so that I named my company The Catch Group. And in that name, I get a constant reminder to carve out time for my values and myself as I build and grow my business.

Three Steps to Boundary Setting

VALUES OF FAMILY, FRIENDSHIP, SELF-CARE, OR HEALTH show up for almost every coaching client I've worked with. Unsurprisingly, these values are often accompanied by feelings of unhappiness or anxiety. They are areas of life that are important but aren't getting prioritized within the schedules of busy executives, parents, and caregivers.

What is holding you back from holding space for yourself? When I ask the women that I coach, the answer that I get most often is "work priorities." That makes sense, as we spend most of our waking time at work, right? Many Americans work many more hours than the old school 9–5. Did people ever really work 9–5? Was that ever really a thing? Many work fifty-plus hours a week, and some much more. That doesn't include commute time, time checking in on email when you are at home, and other small fires you put out.

I'm not going to tell you that I have work-life balance. I don't think that's a thing. I was at a women's conference where speaker Crystal Washington said, "The only people who have work-life balance are work-life balance consultants." It got a laugh from the room filled with over 500 women.

I've found that when I live my life based on my values and create strong value-driven boundaries, I have a values-driven life. How do I prioritize those boundaries and structure my days? You guessed it: through my values. You need to go back to that foundation—your values—to ensure that you actually hold space for your own boundaries. Preserve time and preserve your priorities by holding space for yourself.

The epitome of self-value and worth
is holding space for your own boundaries.

Early in my career, I put in a ton of hours. I, like many new graduates, wanted to prove myself. One of my values is achievement, so I like to drive for results and show impact and get things done. In my early career, I prioritized my value of achievement over others, which meant working too many hours. And that was appropriate in that season of my life for my goals and values.

As my family grew, my value of quality time with them became more and more important to me. In my early mid-career, I was working in a big corporate office, in which face time was particularly emphasized. I had an hour-long commute each day from the house to the office. Living further away from my office was our choice since it was closer to my husband's job, but that meant I would get home after 6:00 p.m. and have a limited amount of time to spend with the baby before we put him to bed.

On days when I could, I started leaving the office early to avoid traffic. Early meant 4:30 p.m., and I would always feel like I had to stealthily leave, making sure to avoid the side of the hallway that had all the executive offices on it. I didn't want senior leaders seeing me leave the office at 4:30 p.m. because I was afraid that they would think I was skipping out or that I wasn't committed to my work. So, I would walk quickly on the other side of the hall, avoid eye contact or any lingering conversations with colleagues as I briskly left.

After exiting the building, it was still a bit of a walk to get to my car in the parking lot. Unavoidably, I'd run into people that were coming into the building as I was leaving for the day.

I'd often get passive-aggressive comments like, "Leaving so soon?" or "Already done for the day?"

But on these days, I would get home in record time. It was glorious. I got to spend more quality time at home with my family, which is what I valued more than anything. I would catch up on email in the evenings. This is an example of the "split shift"—working after the kids go to bed.[9] Many working parents, especially mothers, do this.

It helped me so much that I took action to make it my daily reality. Here's how.

1. Talked to my manager. I decided to have a conversation with him to see if this was a schedule that I could have more frequently. When I say more frequently, I mean that's the new schedule that I wanted every day: to be able to leave between 4:00 and 4:30 p.m. We talked about it, and he was very supportive. Hooray!

2. I followed through consistently. The next thing I needed to do was actually follow my new schedule. It feels like it would be easy to do, but wanting and doing are sometimes very different things. There were days that I needed to get that last thing done. You know that last thing on your list that you think will take five minutes, but when you look at the time, at least twenty minutes has vanished? I

had to not do that last thing sometimes—not have that hallway chat with a friend I wanted to catch up with, or not spend another fifteen minutes responding to emails. Because it was tied to my value of family, it was easier for me to make those decisions day in and day out.

Not only did I have a new schedule, but I benefited from it more than I ever thought that I would. I had more quality time with my family. I spent less time in traffic, which my body thanked me for. And over time, I was able to release the guilt I previously held from "sneaking out."

Now I know that to be successful, I need to set lots of boundaries. I'm most successful in sticking to boundaries when I tie them to something I deeply care about. I root my boundaries in my values.

Rooting them in your values helps you identify the most important boundaries you should be keeping and the motivation to stick to them.

And the next time someone said, "Leaving the office already?" as I was walking out to my car and they were walking back into the office, I would reply back, "Yes, and you're heading in the wrong direction."

Are you headed in the right direction? Here's how to check. The Values First Framework lays out three steps to setting a boundary. Use the accompanying worksheet called **Boundary Builder** from the Values First workbook (download from thecatchgroup. com). The three steps you need to set and keep a boundary are:

1. Tie it to a value.

2. Set up a system.

3. Celebrate consistency.

Time to get started; grab your workbook and a pen. Be honest as you go through the questions. First, prioritize a value that needs a boundary. Not a nice-to-have boundary, but a must-have. To figure out which value to prioritize, refer back to your answers from the **I'm Living My Values When Worksheet.** Prioritize a value that will make the biggest impact on your life and start there. Once you have picked one core value, reflect on the following questions:

- What does it look like to successfully live this core value?

- What's the cost of not doing it?

- What's one thing you can do to make it happen?

By prioritizing a core value and understanding one thing you can do to make it happen, you've just clarified the boundary you need to create. You have identified something that you are probably not doing now to live that core value—a behavior that needs to change. Now you can work towards the desired behavior.

Second, set up a system to support that desired behavior or mindset shift. To identify what needs to happen for you to live that successfully, reflect on the following questions.

- What needs to happen in order for your boundary to work?

- What support do you need?

- What are the internal and external objections?

- How will you deal with boundary objections?

For your boundary to work for you, you may need to have a conversation with your manager, block your calendar, or go to bed at a certain time. You may need more support from others, or to outsource a task to free up more time.

Objections are either internal or external. First, consider the internal objections—the stories that you tell yourself that stop you from setting the boundary in the first place. These are the fears you hold that may not hold any truth, but keep you from exercising the boundary. My internal objections were, "Everyone will think I'm less committed to my job because I'm leaving early," and "I have to be in the office until 5:00 p.m., otherwise I'm not working." These internal objections were things I was telling myself, but were they true? No, they were false. I don't know what other people were thinking about me, and I was working, just in a different way.

Next, consider the external objections. Had anyone told me that I couldn't have this schedule? Nope, the opposite; my manager was very supportive of it. What about those passive-aggressive objections from others as I was leaving the building? I had to make the decision to reject those. Those passive-aggressive people didn't get to set or divert me from my boundaries. What will your strategy be to deal with the boundary objections that you receive?

Know the objections and have an answer or a plan. This isn't about creating a hard line and not being flexible. It is about planning for it when you can and holding to it as much as possible. There will be times when you can't. Give yourself grace and try and be consistent.

The third step in the three-step process is to celebrate consistency. How will you celebrate living your values and consistently holding your boundaries? I rewarded myself with listening to a new book or podcast (yes, I'm a nerd), or fun music I could listen to in the car.

Write a list of things you will do to celebrate. Then do one of the things on your list to reward yourself for keeping to your boundary. Positive reinforcement!

It isn't about beating yourself up for not holding your boundary. It's about celebrating when you do it again and again.

When Your Manager or Company Says No

What if you figure out the boundary that you want, go to your manager to tell them, but the conversation doesn't go well. What if they say no? A leader named Amanda tried to set a boundary and encountered pushback.

Amanda was a manager at a small company. She had a long morning commute—more than an hour and fifteen minutes one-way. After spending her morning in the car, she would get to work feeling frustrated and low on energy. She knew something had to give. Amanda knew that if she checked in on email at home in the morning, she could leave later and miss traffic to get to work a little later in the day. She went to her manager to request her schedule change.

While her manager understood and empathized with her situation, she was not agreeable to Amanda's plan. She told her no. Their team sat next to the CFO, and the optics of showing up that late in the morning wouldn't look good for the team. So she declined Amanda's request. Amanda felt defeated and left the meeting feeling more frustrated.

Amanda thought through her options. In their next one-on-one meeting, Amanda asked her manager if she could come in earlier in the day to arrive at seven, still missing traffic. Her manager agreed to her new solution because she would be seen in the office and get that all-important face time in first thing in the morning.

If you experience a similar situation, how might you be able to move forward? Reflect on the next set of questions to see how you can negotiate for what you value.

- Was there a business reason for the rejection?

- Can a compromise be made?

- Is there a different system that you can set up?

- Go back to the value that boundary is tied to. What other ways can you get that value met?

If your manager consistently turns down your requests or doesn't respect your boundaries, then you may need to evaluate your situation.

- Is this a non-negotiable for you?

- Do you work for a company that doesn't align with your values?

- Is it time to look for a different opportunity that does align with your values?

Reflecting on these questions and taking action will get you one step closer to building boundaries and living a life guided by your values.

Who Are Boundaries For?

Boundaries are for everyone. Boundaries aren't only for people who already have their careers established. They aren't just for executives. They are for all levels of your career or life stage. The earlier you start, the easier it will be to establish a routine and expectation of boundaries in your life. You can create boundaries if you:

- Work in an achievement-driven or competitive company culture

- Are single or have a family

- Have a supportive boss or a jerk for a boss

- Support a leader in a big leadership position

- Don't have a team

- Are out of the workforce

- Are a student

- Are a leader of a team

- Work in a top leadership position

Many women that I coach are in executive roles or have high job aspirations and think they must make big tradeoffs for those top leadership positions. While most of us may have to make some tradeoffs, sometimes it feels like they have to give away their souls for a big job.

It isn't work-life balance. It is setting priorities based on your values. You can have a big job, a big impact, and big boundaries. But you have to build the boundaries. You have to set the priorities. You have to do it consistently.

Non-negotiables

Some boundaries at work are non-negotiables. I had a mentor that told me about being yelled at in a meeting earlier in her career. At the time, she sat through it and didn't say anything. Now, she has a hard line of not tolerating that behavior. If someone yells at her in a meeting, she ends the meeting and leaves the situation.

For me, my safety is non-negotiable. I would often travel for work and get home very late at night. On many occasions, I was by myself in airport parking garages after midnight. The company that I worked for had a maximum you could spend on parking when traveling. I didn't feel safe parking in a general parking lot at the airport when I would have a late return. The company allowed me to expense a taxi ride or use an airport parking valet—both of which were above the allotted parking maximum—when traveling to ensure I felt safe.

What are your non-negotiables?

When Boundaries Are Broken by Others

Even when you have put boundaries in place and have held them consistently, others may not abide by them.

In my mid-career, I was working for a team with multiple clients. Within our workgroup, we valued high-quality work standards, partnership, and collaboration. We set up systems to ensure that we partnered with clients to deliver high-quality work.

We had a client that would often ask for things on his time-frame which, of course, was always immediately. I gave him feedback about how long tasks took, but the very next time, he asked for a favor and an exception. That would mean longer hours for me or my team to accommodate his request, in addition to pushing out other work to get his done first.

I told him we were unable to accommodate his request by his deadline but could get it done by the agreed-upon time, which was three business days later. He didn't like my answer and went to my direct report. My direct report alerted me to the request. I asked her to forward the request to me, and I reiterated to him the answer: no. He went to his manager, who went to my manager. I had anticipated him going around me and had already alerted my manager and prepared him with the email trail. My manager reiterated the timeline to his peer and shut down the expedited request.

People will try and work around your boundary. They may go around you, or above you. Could I have worked longer hours that day to fulfill that request? If we did that for him, then we would have had to do that for everyone, and that wasn't possible. That wouldn't have been following our system or have been in line with our values.

What will you do when—not if, but when—someone breaches your boundary? Here are a few tactics you can use:

- Plan for someone overstepping or breaching your boundary. What will you tell the person that overstepped? Practice the conversation with a trusted friend. Have an email script ready to go so that you can copy and paste it into an email without overthinking it in the moment.

- Overcommunicate your boundary.

- Get air cover from your manager and keep them informed.

- Stay consistent through the discomfort of pushing back.

By preparing for boundary breakdowns, you are setting yourself up to successfully live your values.

Physical Boundaries

THE PHYSICAL ENVIRONMENT AROUND YOU CAN IMPACT your boundaries. A *Wall Street Journal* article from 2020 describes that with no commute, Americans worked more during the pandemic.[10] Many employees traded in their seats on trains or cars for longer hours in their uncomfortable seats at their makeshift work-from-home desks. What was supposed to be temporary ended up being a much more permanent work-from-home situation.

Whether you are a seasoned work-from-home employee or it became your new way of life during the pandemic, boundaries have become more important. How can you create boundaries around work when it is in such close proximity to home life? How do you shut it off when it is right there?

One thing that helped me keep to my boundaries is the way I set up the physical space around me. When creating my workspace at home, it was important that it was clearly delineated and that there was a physical reminder to shut down when work was done. When I "went to work" (upstairs), it signaled to the kids that it was time for me to work and be present there.

They would give me a hug and tell me to have great meetings. It was similar to the goodbyes they previously gave me before I left for the office. Except now, I got to wear stretchy pants and walk up eighteen stairs instead of driving the forty-five minutes to the office. I used to work with a vice president in human resources who, when she worked from home, got dressed as if she were going to the office. This signaled to her children that she was working.

Whether in an office location or working from home, make the space your own. I use this as a way to bring reminders of my values into the spaces where I spend my time while working. In my home office, I have my favorite quotes framed and favorite family pictures hanging on the wall. While I'm on Zoom, the pictures are in the background and often spark conversation, which gives me an opportunity to share some fun memories tied to my values.

Consider the physical space when working from home and boundaries you may need to set.

- Do you have a delineated workspace?

- How will you signal the beginning and end of your workday?

- How can your values be represented in your working space to remind you of your boundaries?

If you find that you're not setting a physical boundary for yourself, go back to the three-step boundary-setting process above in your workbook and take action.

You've learned a simple three-step method to set boundaries. If your boundaries are tied to your values, you're more likely to keep them. It puts a reason behind it—an accountability to prioritize what matters most to you.

Give Yourself Permission to Prioritize You

At eight-and-a-half-months pregnant with my second child, I got a promotion. New job, new boss, transitioning my old role—all while getting ready to have a baby and preparing our first son to be a big brother. It was a lot of change at once. It was great because it was a clean break from my old job to my new job. I transitioned everything before I went on maternity leave and got into my new job for several weeks before baby boy number two arrived.

I took a three-and-a-half-month maternity leave and came back to work ready to prove myself to this new team and to begin to build and lead projects. I felt guilty about getting into a job and then immediately leaving for three and a half months. I didn't want to let them down, so I tried to overcompensate when I got back.

When I took the job, my new boss assured me, "We'll be fine, people have babies all the time. Don't worry about it." It was one of the best things I could have heard at the time (and in my career)—to have my pregnancy supported by another woman that I admired. She made me realize that having a baby and having a big career was possible and that there was no need to apologize for it. But I would be lying if I told you I didn't feel guilt—guilt for taking a job and then being absent to a new team, and guilt for wanting the promotion when it was an important time for my family.

I made the decision to breastfeed, so on the days I was in the office, that meant that I would need to pump. Guess what? Pumping takes time. At a minimum, thirty minutes per session. And I needed to have at least two sessions a day during work hours. So, I prepared for it. I blocked out my schedule for the times I needed to pump during the day. I had all the supplies with me at all times, with spares of everything in my office. My office had glass walls everywhere, so I couldn't pump there. Instead, I went to the lactation room, which was a short walk down the hall.

A lactation space is a room in an office building, mall, or airport that gives people who are breastfeeding a clean space to pump and that has a locked door for privacy. In the lactation room at work, a key was issued from security to enter the room (which we each got to keep for the duration of the time we needed access to the room). When you entered, there were two smaller interior rooms. It was first come, first serve. If the smaller interior rooms were occupied, you had to wait until your fellow working parent left before you could go in and pump.

When I first came back to work, my schedule wasn't very busy. I had flexibility and only a few meetings a day. If the rooms in the lactation space were occupied, I could wait. After a few weeks of getting into my new role, though, my calendar began to fill up. I still had time blocked for my pumping sessions during the day, but if I went in and a room wasn't available, I had to wait or find an alternative place to pump.

I've pumped in bathrooms (gross), my car (multiple times), or office rooms that I could barricade or block so no one could come in. Only once did someone actually get through my makeshift barricade at an offsite meeting when I was pumping. I affixed a sign on a scrap piece of paper, scrawling "occupied" in green highlighter and put it on the exterior side of the door and had put a heavy chair on the other side of the door. If someone missed the sign, they would be stopped by the chair in front of the door. Just in case, I had a cover on while pumping. Even with all of those deterrents, it was pretty awkward to meet a new team member when she went looking for someone and came into the room, totally missing my sign, undeterred by the chair barricade.

Once in a while, I made the decision not to pump. If you miss a pump, you are messing with your milk production and you may produce less, which isn't great because it's a supply and demand thing. If you skip a pump, you are telling your body that you don't need to produce that milk for your baby, and you then may produce less over time. I wasn't producing as much milk as I wanted anyway, so missing a pumping session was not ideal, and the guilt piled on.

Over time, my job got more demanding, and I made tradeoffs. I didn't pump for as long as I should have. I took calls while I was pumping. And sometimes I took meetings instead of pumping. Then I took more meetings. My twice-daily pumping would be compromised to one pump a day. And then that pump would happen later and later each day. And then sometimes I would get home and the baby would have already eaten, and I had to pump then instead of feeding him. I didn't keep my schedule blocked and held for pumping. I made small decisions to be available for a meeting (instead of pumping), and eventually it led to me stop pumping and feeding him breast milk because I hadn't held on to my boundaries. The boundary of keeping my time blocked for pumping had a longer-term consequence.

I fed him breast milk for ten and a half months, and I'm proud of that. Did he get supplemented with formula? Yep! Does it matter? NOPE. It's easy to see how a boundary can get overridden because of the demands or priorities of something else.

In hindsight, instead of giving myself permission to miss my pumping sessions, I could have given myself permission to de-cline a meeting invitation that was clearly labeled "busy" on my calendar. By accepting meeting invitations, I was saying yes to someone else and no to myself.

I could have said yes to myself more to keep my boundary.

I didn't want to seem unavailable to others. I didn't want to seem uncommitted. But those are the exact things that I was being to myself—uncommitted and unavailable. In that moment, though, giving myself grace and compassion for doing what I could do at the time was the most important gift I could give myself.

What I know is that to be relentless with boundaries, you have to keep space for them.

Living your boundaries looks like:

- Telling people about your boundaries

- Telling them again

- Modeling the behavior for your team

- Empowering others to live their boundaries

- Saying no

- Saying no and offering an alternative solution

- Feeling uncomfortable

- Feeling uncomfortable but doing it anyway

- Having hard discussions

- Delegating

- Being relentlessly consistent

- Giving yourself permission to be committed and available to your own interests above others' interests

By modeling it, you can set the expectation and give others permission to put boundaries around their work too. Sometimes others need to see something happening before they believe that they can do it. Then they are empowered to do it for themselves. When you are in a leadership position, I think it's even more important to role model.

Keeping your boundaries looks like saying no. A lot. Or, saying no and setting a realistic expectation of what can happen. It looks like saying no to meeting requests, declining them, or giving alternate times that you can meet. It means telling people what you are doing, and then doing it consistently. My client, Megan, had to learn to say no to others to say yes to herself.

Megan was a tenured executive in the hospitality industry. She was in back-to-back meetings every day and was overwhelmed. Upon reflection of her values, she realized that her value of achievement and knowledge—being seen as an expert and contributor at work—was leaving her exhausted.

She was giving so much of her energy to her job that when she did have family time and downtime, she was too exhausted to enjoy it. Her values of achievement and knowledge were impeding on successfully living her value of family.

What did successfully living her value of family mean? She wanted to spend focused time with her child. She knew she needed a leave from work to accomplish this. The company she worked for reflected values of showing care to employees first. This was very personal. Would her manager understand? Would her company support this leave?

She worried about the objections she may receive. Would she still be seen as the expert if she wasn't available? Megan built a system to prepare her team for her absence, including a plan to reprioritize meetings and delegate to her team. Then, she had the discussion with her manager about her needs.

Guess what happened? Her manager was very supportive. Megan was able to spend that focused time with her family. What if she hadn't shared this information with her company? She'd be unavailable for her family and potentially unhappier, unable to get that need met.

When delivering the message to her team that she would be taking a leave, she got unexpected reactions. They thanked her. They thanked her for showing up as an example of the company's values of caring for employees. They had never seen it in action with such a senior leader. It motivated them to think about their needs too. What could be possible for them?

Living your boundaries means being okay with the uncomfortable feeling that you get when you keep your boundary. You may feel uncomfortable asserting your boundaries. You may feel like you are letting someone down. For years, your go-to behavior has been to show up for others first. The discomfort that you are feeling is discomfort from building a new behavior. This new behavior conflicts with the years of people-pleasing behaviors— of being available for everyone else. Know that this momentary discomfort in upholding your boundaries will bring you the peace that you need in time.

Your long-term peace is greater than the short-term discomfort.

Keeping your boundaries looks like prioritizing something and deprioritizing something else—saying no to a good idea. There are projects that you get so excited about, you don't care if you work more on them because it's fun and energizing work, but it is still more work. I've had to say no to some of this work. Because time is a limited commodity, what would we have to give up to work on this new shiny project?

It is in the everyday that you live your values and boundaries. The everyday decisions. Do I attend a client meeting, or do I delegate it so I can work on a prioritized project? Do I go to a networking meeting, or do I keep my workout plans? By holding to your boundaries, you are creating an environment of living your values to prioritize what is important to you.

It doesn't always feel good. But you have to be consistent. If you don't stick to your boundaries, then no one else will.

Jet Setting and Boundary Setting

IN MY EXPERIENCE, AND IN TALKING TO MY CLIENTS, ONE OF the hardest places to make and keep boundaries is during work travel. When you travel, your schedule is disrupted. You can't always control your physical surroundings or your environment. Your usual routine is interrupted with new time zones and a varied schedule.

Throughout my career, my job has required a certain percentage of travel. Committee meetings, conferences, and events were part of the package deal in consulting and corporate life. The days were long and full of events. These trips can be daunting to an introvert because you are "on" all day long. I've learned from trial and error (and even more error) what works to maintain my energy levels. Many of these things are learned from my personal experience or watching seasoned travel warriors and trying some of their strategies.

All of these tips have something in common: creating boundaries. To be at my best on these trips, I need to dig into my values of achievement, growth, and development. Here's how you can do that.

Make a Plan Before You Go

First things first: know what you are getting into for every trip.

- *Review the meeting agenda.* Review the meeting agenda to understand time commitments and the number of meetings and events. If there is no agenda, don't go on the trip.

- *Decide what you are not participating in.* Look at the overall schedule to see what is mandatory and which engagements you can decline. If there are events from 7:00 a.m. to 10:00 p.m. each day for four days in a row, it may not be sustainable for you to attend everything. Which events are the most important, and which ones are optional? Figure out which ones you won't be attending in advance and set expectations ahead of time, if needed. This is an example of setting a boundary to protect balance and maintain energy.

- *Schedule your existing boundaries into your agenda.* For example, plan out which days you will be working out, and schedule that in the morning. A sign of not maintaining that boundary might mean bringing home clean workout clothes (that could count as weightlifting because you did carry them around in your suitcase, after all).

Meals When Traveling

I have spent a lot of time in meetings in hotel conference rooms or ballrooms with table rounds. In the mornings, there is usually a buffet at the hotel, where you grab your plate of food, find coffee, and then sit down in open seating in a big room. It reminds me of the first day of school at lunch when you are trying to figure out where to sit. In the room, there are clients and there are colleagues from the organization. There are some tables with a few people, and others with none. My secret wish would be to go sit down at a table *all.by.my.self.* Or to sit down at a table with a few people whom I already know. But to build new relationships, that means spending time with people I've not met before.

It's an interesting challenge of eating my eggs, not getting salsa on my white blouse, and also saying something witty to someone I don't know very well—all before I've had coffee. In these situations, I scan the room. Is there a friendly face to sit by? Is there a new table that I can start where others can join me?

I find a table and ask the standard, "Is anyone sitting here?" to the people at the table. I get the usual, "Yes, you are!" followed by the obligatory chuckle. Then the small talk ensues in between taking bites of fresh fruit and looking for almond milk for my coffee. *Where are you from? How was your travel in?* My go-to plan is to ask questions and get someone else talking. I'm a great listener, and it also reserves some energy for the rest of the day.

After lots of breakfasts like this, I've found that some of them drain my energy that I need for that morning's meeting. Here are a few ways that I've maintained my energy and hunger levels while on the road:

- *Eat before going to a networking event.* This is something I learned from a CEO that I worked for. He knew that he would be having multiple conversations with people and wouldn't get a chance to eat a full meal, so he would eat before he got to the event so he wouldn't be hungry and wouldn't be caught at the end of the night without eating anything substantial. I started doing this for breakfast.

- *Pack your favorite breakfast in luggage.* When I travel, I try to pack the stuff I need for my morning protein shake so I can drink it in my room. I bring my Blender bottle and protein powder and grab almond milk from the store the night before so I can make sure I have my breakfast before I leave my room. Then I join everyone at the buffet and get coffee. Joining a table to grab a coffee seems more approachable to me. When I'm in full introvert mode, I'll even skip joining a table and just get my coffee to go.

- *Set up breakfast meetings in advance.* I like to set up breakfast meetings in advance, so I can have breakfast with a smaller group of people but also get some business done, too. These meetings can be used to work through an agenda topic, or sometimes they are truly just a catch-up with a stakeholder. These one-on-one breakfasts or small group breakfasts give me energy, since I love to build relationships one-on-one and truly make a connection with people before starting my day of full meetings.

Recharging through the Day

If you've held to your boundaries as you've gone through your travel day, maybe you've already worked out, had a protein shake, and caught up with a stakeholder—all before the first meeting of the day has started. That gives you the energy that you need to be present in the meeting, facilitating, listening, processing, and contributing. Here are a few ways to maintain your energy throughout the day.

- *Take time for yourself at lunch.* I ensure that I take at least ten to fifteen minutes to recharge at lunch. Usually that looks like walking around the building or outside, if weather permits. I try to do this with a colleague to catch up, or sometimes by myself. At lunch, there's usually another buffet situation. If that's the case, I power through that, and then try to get back to the meeting room a bit early to collect my thoughts before the next agenda item.

- *Rest after meetings end, before dinner.* After the meeting ends for the day, typically at 5:00 or 5:30 p.m., there is a bit of time—usually less than an hour—before reconvening for networking or dinner. This is the MOST important recharge. You will be tempted to go back to your room and start churning through the emails that have gone unread because you've been in meetings all day. There will always be email waiting for you, or another thing to do. The most important thing I need to do is rest. What does this recharge time look like for you?

Recharge time for me is doing something mindless. Sometimes I literally lay down. Other times I watch thirty minutes of bad cable TV or Netflix. There is nothing better than catching an episode of the original *Law & Order i*n your hotel room—nothing better; you cannot convince me otherwise. The successful outcome I'm looking for here is mindlessness. Some may call that escapism—whatever, that is what I need. After thirty minutes of emptying my mind, I eat a granola bar (remember, eat before you go to dinner!) and then change into whatever I need to for dinner and make my way to the next event.

End of the Day Energy

You've made it to the end of the day, and hopefully you've put in boundaries to conserve your energy and attention span. You may still have a networking event or dinner to attend, and you most likely still need to be "on." Here are some strategies to stay at your best, even at the end of a long day of meetings.

- *Know what food or alcohol will do to your energy level.* At work events, I used to have a rule for myself for one drink at cocktail hour and one drink with dinner. Now I try not to drink at all, because it sucks my energy and makes me tired. My drink of choice is sparkling water with lime. After so many years of work travel and evening functions as part of human resources and senior leadership, I've seen a lot of people do not-so-great things when alcohol is part of the equation at work functions.

- *Have an exit plan.* I know this will be shocking to hear, but when dinner is over, I generally get back to my hotel as soon as humanly possible. I love a good conversation over dinner, but by this point I'm exhausted and need to wind down and get ready for the next day. Places you will not find me: at the dinner table, lingering, or the hotel bar for after-dinner drinks. Do I have FOMO (fear of missing out)? Nope. I have what introverts call JOMO—the joy of missing out. Will it be hard for you to leave? If so, grab a work buddy and make a plan in advance to both leave at the same time.

- *Stick to your sleep schedule.* At the end of the day, you'll most likely need to check in on email, but don't go down the black hole and stay up for hours working. You need your sleep. Plug me in; I need to recharge.

By keeping your boundaries while you travel, you can maintain your energy levels and show up as the leader you want to be.

Through this section, you have experienced the power of setting and keeping boundaries, and you have practiced the three-step process of tying your boundaries to your values. And hopefully, I've convinced you to try out rowing or whatever your mindfulness alternative may be.

Now, you are going to learn about how Uplifting Others is part of your values-first life. Let's start by finding your team—your Catch Crew—that models their values and keeps their boundaries intact.

Uplifting Others

Uplifting Others

Find the support you need from peers and mentors to keep your boundaries intact, and learn strategies to model your values with your team by building a Values First culture as a leader.

Values First Framework *from The Catch Group*

Accountability
through Others

ONE OF THE BEST WAYS TO BE CONSISTENT IN LIVING YOUR
values is through the accountability of others and empowering
others through your actions. In the Uplifting Others section of
the Values First Framework, you will identify your support network and plan for the culture you want to build for your team
aligned to your values.

One of the best ways that I've been consistent in living my
values is through the accountability of peers.

Peer pressure is usually labeled as a bad thing. I'm not talking
about the "if your friend jumped off a bridge, would you?" kind
of peer pressure. I'm talking about peers as accountability partners.
Having an accountability partner that you trust, that isn't your
manager or mentor, who doesn't have hierarchical or perceived
power over you, can be very beneficial.

When I'm thriving at work, it is usually when I have a close
peer circle. Trust built within a peer group at work or outside of
work is an immeasurable asset.

I met Kristen at a work function in my corporate job. We were
in Tucson, Arizona, training some managers, and we bonded at a

Dave & Busters over bad food and talking about our dating lives. We grew our careers at the company together. She was ahead of me, guiding me along the way, offering sage advice and a safe space to vent or to get feedback. We trusted each other, and the best part was that we trusted each other to give hard messages.

When Kristen needed to hear a hard message, she would sometimes count on me to tell her my honest opinion of something. My husband often reminds me that he's never left guessing about what I think—in a lovingly joking way—because it is usually easy to know where I stand on an issue. You can see it on my face, or if you can't, then I'm probably going to tell you how I feel about it directly. After a meeting with one of her clients, I was in Kristen's office, and she mentioned that she was always stuck taking notes in this recurring meeting. She said that it made her feel like she wasn't an equal in the meeting.

"What would happen if you didn't take the meeting notes?" I asked.

"Well, someone has to take the meeting notes. I mean, isn't it my job to take the meeting notes?" she asked.

"Is it your job to take the meeting notes?" I asked.

"I mean, no one else has volunteered," she said.

"Do you always volunteer?" I asked.

"I usually just do it," she said.

"What impact might that have?" I asked.

"That I'm doing the administrative stuff," she said.

"Kristen, you are known for your credibility, influencing senior leaders, and your dedication to the work. You are amazing at your job. Stop taking the notes in meetings. Just stop and see what happens. Create impact with your strategy, not your detailed notetaking ability."

Kristen would later be one of my biggest supporters and a champion for me to get a big promotion. She's given me encouragement, direct feedback, and has celebrated my successes.

This friendship, and peer accountability in general, is something that I consider part of my values of growth and development. Having a trusted peer in the workplace is also a sign of success. When I don't have it, I feel lost. At the beginning in a new job, it is much harder because I don't have that support system built in—because I haven't built the relationships yet. Instead, I rely on my external support network of peers that I've built during my career.

Renae has been my peer accountability partner since the beginning of my career. In my first job, she was on the hiring team that hired my cohort. I hadn't met her until I started, and she had been with that company for three years. That was a lifetime in that company.

She was tenured, knew what she was doing with clients, and was managing many of my peers. I tried to learn from her as much as I could. She ended up moving to the Midwest, but then back to Texas for another job after we all left that company. She and I ended up working together at a different organization later in our careers.

She's a confidante and an amazing friend who tells me what I need to hear, even when it isn't what I want to hear. She knows what I need to do to get my butt in gear and stop feeling sorry for myself. She coaches me through tough situations without judgment, by asking me the right questions to keep me moving forward.

Trusted peer relationships have been vital to my success and growth.

Blind Spots

Even if you have clarity in your values, sometimes feedback is right in front of your face, and you can't see it—you have a blind spot. Once, I was rolling out a big employee survey that was sent out to thousands of employees to complete. It was an optional survey to fill out, but the company wanted high response rates; it was important for them to hear from every associate on how they were doing as an organization and what they could do to get better. We usually had a themed marketing campaign to increase awareness of the survey during the weeks it was open for collecting responses.

We were just coming off an election year in the United States, and we thought we'd play into the theme of voting for the marketing campaign. Filing out your survey was like casting your vote. We used the tagline "Your vote counts!" to promote the survey through digital signage, posters, videos, and emails while the survey administration window was open for employees to complete. In one of our weekly meetings, I was excited to show my manager, Jeff, one of the poster designs. The vendor used a part of the company logo for the "o" in the word "counts."

After one look at the sign, Jeff's face was so red I thought he was choking. He couldn't catch his breath. He was dying of laughter and wasn't making eye contact with me. I didn't understand.

"What?" I asked, perplexed. "What is it?"

"You don't see it?" he coughed out in between breaths of laughter.

"No, I don't see it."

"I can't say it out loud," he barely got the words out. "Take out the logo and read it."

I covered up the logo acting as the "o" on the poster with my finger. *Oh, dear God. Your vote c*unts.* Not exactly what we were going for. My naïve human resources mind hadn't seen it.

That poster didn't make it in the campaign. Thank God I got the unfiltered feedback from him. Not that he could have held back that feedback. Also, it turns out that using the logo as a letter was outside of our brand standards, and we wouldn't have been able to use it anyway. We decided to go with another version of the poster design instead. Easiest decision ever.

That feedback was something I literally didn't see, and it was right in front of my eyes. I was just reading over it, literally. Definition of blind spot. Luckily, this feedback example was humorous and easily fixed, but sometimes blind spots are more harmful, and your trusted relationships will be there to support you through it while giving you accountability to live up to your values.

Sometimes we have obvious opportunities and need people like Renae and Kristen to help us through. Other times we need people like Jeff to help us see what we can't.

Building Your Catch Crew

KNOWING THE PEOPLE IN YOUR LIFE WHO WILL HOLD YOU accountable to your values makes you feel less alone, more supported, and better able to hold your boundaries. So, let's build your Catch Crew™.

Have you ever taken an employee survey that asks you if you have a best friend at work? It may feel weird to be asked that. Why would your company ask you something like that? Because it is tied to performance. Employees who have a best friend at work have higher workplace engagement.[11] More engagement usually means higher performance from employees. That is beneficial for both the company that you work for and for you.

You may have a best friend at work. If you are anything like me, there may not be just one person. There is a crew, a group of people that you go to for different perspectives. These are trusted peers that you can confide in and who confide in you. Let's brainstorm who is in your Catch Crew.

Get your workbook and write out a list of people you go to for any of the situations below. Individuals in your Catch Crew don't have to work with you but should be peers. They may be a colleague at a previous office, or a dear friend from college. Members of your Catch Crew may be individuals who:

- You go to lunch with.

- You talk to explicitly in emojis.

- You hype up, or who hype you when you have a bad day.

- You always need to catch up with on how your weekends went.

- You go to vent to.

- You ask for feedback from.

- You give feedback to.

- You feel safe around.

- You tell about your promotion first.

- You check in with after a hard day.

- You talk to about career issues.

- You confide in about your horrible manager.

- You know well and admire their boundaries.

When you are finished, look at that list; you have a great group of people that support you and that you support. Next, send your Catch Crew some love. Send each one of them an individual note or text to thank them for something, or just to let them know that you were thinking about them. Tell them what you value about them.

Now that you've figured out who is there to support you, let's discover how you can help others live their values.

Supporting Others

Early in my career, I worked for a small consulting business, and we found out layoffs were imminent. It was only a matter of time until I would be laid off, and eventually I was. I ended up in a better culture, working in a corporate environment. My new manager was Arlene. She was direct but patient. She had a positive outlook and high standards for her team. She expressed her expectations easily. Being the people pleaser that I was (and still am), I wanted to do an amazing job for her.

One of the first things she delegated to me was a summary of an internal diversity and inclusion survey. I spent hours reviewing the open-ended comments to show her what a great and thorough job I could do. I made a five-page PowerPoint presentation and gave it to her a few days later. I was impressed with my conscientious self and knew that I'd delivered a masterpiece of a first project to her.

As I was reviewing themes from the open-ended comments, she came by my cubicle. I had papers spread everywhere—like, the whole thing was covered. I had printed out every comment and was sorting them into different "piles" of sentiments from employees. I was in the middle of the project when I left for the day. I knew I would return to this important project first thing the next day. It was as if I had walked away and was coming back, but in between I went home.

The next morning my oh-so-direct manager stopped by. "Oh hey, you might want to clean up your desk before you leave for the day. Especially if there is sensitive information on your desk. We have a clean desk policy here."

Like a deer in headlights, I looked at her and said, "Sure, of course. No problem."

Was there any private information on my desk? I am, after all, a human resource professional. A clean desk policy? What the heck is that? Basically, *don't be a slob* is what I took away from this exchange. From then on, of course, I cleaned up my desk before I left for the day. More importantly, there was never confidential employee information left out in the open.

I sent her my five-page PowerPoint masterpiece, and she gave me feedback in the most patient way.

"This is a great first draft, but can you get it to one page?" she asked.

Wow, one page. I didn't even think about the length. How could I fit all this amazingness onto one page? I thought.

"Otherwise," she said, "the client may not read it all, and they'll lose the great insights."

My summary was, in fact, longer than the actual survey. That is the amazingness of Arlene. She valued my effort and coached me on what the business expected. I respected everything about her approach.

A few months later, we were working to get a meeting with some key leaders to discuss a project that would include multiple departments. I looked at our calendars and couldn't find anything during the timeframe that would work. That week, I found out later, was back-to-school time. At the time, I was dating my boyfriend (who would eventually become my husband), but I didn't have children. I had no awareness of this time of year since I'd been out of school for so long and didn't think of my time in semesters anymore. I was trying to get the meeting scheduled and went to Arlene with frustration.

"Push it to the next week" she said. "It's back-to-school time; we need to work around people's schedules—they want to take their kids to the first day of school." I was mildly annoyed by this. *Isn't work more important than that,* I thought? To me, this meeting was more important, but to everyone else, no, it wasn't. Of course it wasn't. Arlene, the patient person that she was, reminded me how important it is to be there for events.

To show my regret for not realizing how important this was, I said, "Man, I'm such a retard."

She immediately, ever so nicely, without missing a beat said, "I don't think you should use that word. It can be offensive to people who are differently abled." I was mortified. She must have hated me. I prided myself on advocating for others. It was one of my core values. I didn't understand kids (wanting to schedule a meeting during back-to-school), and now I was most likely offending someone. How many times had I said that word? Not speaking anymore sounded like the right thing to do, so I wouldn't mess anything else up. I was embarrassed and knew I was wrong to say it.

I didn't realize the significance of that conversation—the courage that it takes to have a conversation like that, to call someone out. I realized just how hard it was, how awkward, when I started having similar conversations. It is a skill that needs to be practiced, but you should do it even when it is awkward or uncomfortable. When I talked to people I loved who said it, they'd reply that "they didn't mean anything by it." When I would awkwardly call it out, they might say something like, "Oh, you're being too sensitive. I didn't mean it like that." Even though that wasn't their intent, the impact on others could be big.

The feedback that Arlene gave me was her living her values, her principles. She showed me what integrity looked like. If you're not sure about something, say something. Don't ever cover up anything or shove it down; let it see the light, and you'll never do wrong.

As a leader, it is important to live my values within my leadership style. That means modeling my values. When you are in a leadership role, people are watching what you do. They are watching what you say and how you react. They are watching what you react to and how long it takes. They don't get to see the full context of the decisions that you make. Often, they only see the outcome.

Leading can be lonely and hard, which is why it is important to me to belong to an organization that is aligned with my values. For instance, my value of advocacy is important to me; I want to work at an organization that advocates for diverse representation in all roles of an organization through a diversity, equity, and inclusion strategy. It is motivating for me to work for someone that leads in alignment with their values. My values and my manager's values don't have to be the same. But I need to see that they are aligned with the organization's culture and that they are living their own values.

As a leader, you need to show up with grace and consistency. What does that do? It shows the behavior you want to model and shows that it is permissible. It gives them permission to do something similar.

In my corporate job, we transitioned to a more casual dress code. We had been business casual, except for jeans on Fridays. We could "dress for our day," meaning that if we did not have a customer meeting, we could wear jeans on any day. The senior teams were to model the behavior to show that it was acceptable. Some had an extremely hard time doing that. They looked visibly uncomfortable showing up to the office in jeans. Many did not even wear jeans on a Friday when it was allowed. But they did their best and showed up modeling the behavior.

If employees do not see you doing it, then they may not think it is okay for them to do it. They may just think it is a trend or something for the younger workforce. To change the culture, it takes showing up for something consistently in order to make that change. What behaviors from your **I'm Living My Values Worksheet** (from the Values First section) will show up at work? Who will see them? How can you ensure that you'll be consistent?

For me, the indicators of success for my family absolutely show up at work. People will see when I am or am not in the office. They will see if I attend meetings when I am supposed to be with my kids. If I'm maintaining balance, I bet I'm showing up as a better leader for my people with less frustration and anxiety. I bet I'm a better coach. I bet I am a better listener. The weeks that I get my workout in more days and set my pace for the week will most likely show in all aspects of my life, especially at work. But the long game—the consistency of that—is where I want to be able to see the outputs. I want to see what impact my behavior has on the culture of my team, and the boundaries that they set and live by.

As a leader, I think you also need to talk about your values transparently. When I started in my C-suite job, I set up one-on-one meetings with each person from the team to get to know them. This was a suggestion from my direct report, Tonya (the most thoughtful gift-giver who's ever lived), who did that when she came into the organization a few months prior. No one had done that previously with this team before she did. I had some of the best conversations in those Zoom meetings. I started by bringing everyone through the values on my vision board in a team meeting and let them know that I'd be having informal conversations with each of them in the upcoming weeks. We were able to connect on values as a starting point.

In some of the meetings, the team members put together a similar PowerPoint page as a response to mine, so I could get to know them at that level, too. It was heartwarming to see their families, their goals, their visions, and their values depicted on a page in a visual way. Each person is unique with multiple experiences. I was in awe of the life stories and capabilities that they were each bringing to their work. This gave me time to form a personal connection to each of them early in my tenure in the role and organization. It also set the stage for talking about modeling behavior I wanted for my life and team.

In my life, there are few better examples of someone modeling their values than my friend Kiva.

Kiva, an unassumingly funny, stunning woman and the most amazing mother I've ever met, joined our small but mighty workgroup in my early-mid career. We became fast friends at work, bonding over stories of her family, fashion, and recipes. We also bonded over similar negative interactions with a male colleague, John. John managed up very well. But somehow, he always needed something, urgently. Whenever he emailed or called, it was always something—something that he was usually delegating to one of us, on his impossible deadline.

We had a department meeting every year to celebrate the year's accomplishments. There was a banquet night for the formal awards. The most coveted award that was given out was The Eagle. The Eagle award was given under different categories, but the gist was that the recipient of The Eagle had gone above and beyond, and their work had resonated beyond their team and department to impact the company in some way. It was a crystal Eagle that sat on a wood base. It was a fun night to cheer on your colleagues while eating the sad hotel-cheesecake dessert.

Guess who got an Eagle award that night? John! We were floored, like, *huh?* What or whom did John fool to get this award? Whom did he mow down to impress? Needless to say, it was a bit demotivating to see his behavior being rewarded.

On the following Monday, Kiva and I had to catch up about this tragedy. Not a real tragedy, but one of those times when you don't think karma is working at all. At the end of our discussion, we decided that we needed to create a new award since, you know, the Eagle award was obviously rigged. That was the day that the Peacock award was built using Google images of a peacock on a certificate we made in PowerPoint. From that day on, we'd print out the PowerPoint page and give each other the Peacock award to show appreciation for each other. We cheered each other on enough that Peacock became our nickname for each other.

Kiva celebrated others better and with more enthusiasm than anyone I've ever known. She always volunteered to plan and celebrate everyone she loved. If there was a baby shower, she'd plan the menu and the decorations. If there was a wedding shower, she'd meticulously plan the games. She lived for celebrating others, especially her family.

One of my favorite parties was the high school graduation of her daughter. She had purple and gold popcorn, themed food, and the best iced tea I've ever tasted. My sister and I attended to offer our congratulations to the graduate. Kiva beamed, in her entertaining element, spending time and laughing with her guests, who were all important to her. They felt important, and she made us feel welcomed, everywhere she was. That was the last time I got to celebrate with her. She passed away unexpectedly later that year.

The value of celebrating and appreciation lives on with everyone that she loved. She was a constant cheerleader, celebrating small moments, large moments, Peacock moments. In my career, I continued our tradition. I created a departmental award called The Peacocks, in which I recognized nominated team members who demonstrated and lived the strategy of our team, above and beyond. The Peacock awards lived on, celebrating the successes of people that Kiva had never known, but whose leadership lessons they were lucky to receive.

What kind of legacy do you want to leave?

Living a values-first life and modeling your values is a great way to positively impact the world and inspire those around you.

Next, let's talk about how your values and boundaries influence those around you. Courtney thought her values of quality, knowledge, and gratitude were the reasons her team was high performing.

Build Your Team Culture

I COACHED A LEADER NAMED COURTNEY, AN EXECUTIVE IN finance, who was working to advance her career. She wanted to get to another level in her organization and to become a more inspirational leader. She identified her values and prioritized high quality. She had high standards for her work and that of her team. She told me about a complex report that she would run every week, which left her unable to take much time off. It was so valued by her peers that she didn't want to delegate it to anyone else.

Knowledge, another core value, was important to Courtney. This showed up as being available when others needed her and being an expert in her field. She mentioned that she was working on disconnecting. She had recently gone to the beach for a four-day family reunion and didn't take her laptop—a big win for her. I asked her how it went for her team in her absence. She mentioned that there were a few hiccups and she had to do some cleanup when she was back that wouldn't have happened if she were there to resolve it in real time.

Courtney also had a core value of gratitude. She often cc'd the CEO of the company on notes of gratitude and thanks to her team to give them visibility. In her employee engagement survey, her employees noted that she often personally reached out to them to thank them for their contributions to the organization's goals.

Upon review of her values and leadership style, Courtney reflected on the culture she was setting for her team. By always being available and checking in with her direct reports (and not delegating important tasks), she realized that it may look like she didn't trust her team. By working longer hours, she had created an "always on" culture, even though she didn't expect them to work the same number of hours. The gratitude she showed her team had extended to a team member suggesting a way to highlight "going above and beyond" for each other during their monthly team meetings.

She saw how her values and boundaries, or lack thereof, had created her current team culture. She knew she needed to make some intentional changes to build the culture to not only motivate, but care for her team.

What culture are you creating with your values and boundaries? Go to your workbook to the **Culture Builder Worksheet** to reflect on the culture that you create in the teams that you lead. It doesn't matter if you are a leader of a big organization or if you don't have any direct reports. You can build a culture of your values within your leadership style regardless of your role in the organization.

1. *Self-reflection.* List your core values and the boundaries that are associated with those. Answer the following questions.

   * What impact do my boundaries have on my team?

   * How does my lack of boundaries impact my team?

   * What informal ways do I reward my team based on my values?

- What formal ways do I reward my team based on my values?

- How do I spend time with my team members each week (one-on-one meetings, team meetings, etc.)?

2. *Get feedback.* Ask your team for their candid feedback on those questions. You can do that informally in a one-on-one meeting. Write a quick note, telling them that you are reading this book and wanted to get their feedback in your next one-on-one meeting. Conversely, you can ask your human resources business partner, manager, or someone in your Catch Crew at your organization to send these out on your behalf via email. Direct reports can respond directly back to them to keep it confidential. Or have someone set up a confidential survey for you.

3. *Take action.* Don't ask for feedback if you aren't going to do anything with it. Ensure you act on at least one thing from the feedback. Let your Catch Crew, your manager, and your direct reports know what you are working on and ensure you follow up on progress.

Here are a few example action items to build a culture based on your values and boundaries.

- Set core working hours for your team.

- Put a no-Friday-meeting policy in place.

- Model not calling in for meetings when you are on vacation.

- Set up a new formal recognition program.

- Set up flexible working arrangements and model them (in the office some days, working from home on others).

- Be consistent with your one-on-ones with your direct reports, and don't cancel them.

- Write informal notes of gratitude on real paper and send them.

- Delegate tasks to direct reports to give them visibility and deprioritize something else for them so it isn't just more work.

- Invest in development for the team on something they all want to get better at.

- Ask for feedback often.

- Be transparent about what skills you are developing for yourself and how you are doing that.

- Better yet, work with your team to co-create a list of culture builders and ways of working.

By modeling your values and boundaries with your team, you can create a high-performing culture that motivates and empowers your team to live a life of their values, while setting and keeping their boundaries.

Through Uplifting Others, you now understand the value of peer pressure and peer feedback, have made a list of people who can support you and whom you support in living values, and know how to build a culture to inspire and motivate others through your values.

Now let's talk about when conflict arises, because inevitably it will.

Experiencing Conflict

Experiencing Conflict

Create a plan now so when conflict arises with yourself or your team, you can easily know what to avoid and how to move forward in alignment with your values.

Values First Framework *from The Catch Group*

Standing Up for Your Values

THERE WILL BE TIMES WHEN YOU AREN'T LIVING YOUR VALUES, when your priorities will be out of alignment. It will happen, but in the Experiencing Conflict section of the Values First Framework, I'm giving you tools and resources to deal with conflicts and boundary breaches when you are in situations misaligned with your values.

Living your values every day will give you a way to create boundaries, draw lines in the sand, and set priorities. Along with those priorities will come difficult decisions and hard conversations. Sometimes people may not be open to your decisions, or it will be hard for them to understand your decisions. You will find yourself in situations where you need to stand up for yourself or others, based on the values that you hold.

During a business trip early in my career, I was traveling with two colleagues, Rachel and Bob. Rachel had a no-nonsense attitude, with a sharp wit. Bob was a quintessential small-town family man with salt and pepper hair, who spoke with a Midwestern accent. Rachel was at a similar age and stage in her career as I was, while Bob was at a later stage in his professional life and had recently transitioned careers. He was relatively new in our industry, and we were all peers.

We were onsite to do some work at one of our client's offices. My colleagues and I had flown in the night before, and the clients also flew in from their home office for the meetings. We were scheduled to meet in the hotel for breakfast to go over logistics and plan out our work for the week. This was the first time we would meet this client in person.

We arrived early and looked around the open seating for a table big enough to accommodate us. A family had come into the breakfast area at the same time, also looking to find a seat, getting ready for their day on what I presumed was a family vacation. Our clients were two men in their mid-careers, dressed in the pre-requisite khaki pants and button-down shirts that scream business casual, with belts matching their shoes. We introduced ourselves to the clients and sat down.

At the table, I sat in between my two colleagues, facing our clients on the other side of the table. Just beyond them was my view of the coffee station and the spread of complimentary hotel breakfast including the usual suspects of oatmeal, cereal, bagels, and—if you wanted to wait the five minutes for it to cook—the crown jewel of the breakfast array, the waffle station.

Breakfast was included in our rate at the hotel. We had a per diem rate for travel and expenses (a capped rate of what was reimbursable per day for food on a business trip). If you went over your limit, you wouldn't get reimbursed, so having breakfast included in our hotel rate meant that I could have a nicer dinner with my colleagues later, and maybe even a glass of wine. Another strategy is to not spend your per diem at all and get that money back—always a fun game to play on a long business trip when you are early in your career.

We started with introductions and a little small talk about our flights and our night's sleep at this chain hotel. We sipped our coffee and nibbled on our breakfasts at our too-crammed table of drinks and half-eaten bagels, with our notebooks propped on our laps ready to take notes about the logistics of our meetings for the week. We were about to get into the details—you know, the moment where you switch from small talk to the actual agenda and important topics—when Bob said to our clients, "Well, you can see how pretty these girls are, now they can show you how smart they are."

Awkward silence ensued. I was livid. My body temperature rose at least five degrees. My eyes darted to Bob, then to Rachel, then back to Bob, then to the clients, then down. *What the actual hell did he just say?* I had zero words in that moment. I felt small, but had a rage building inside. Pretty first, then prove your worth. It felt like the patriarchy was speaking through him directly into my soul in that moment.

In the past, these moments had felt sneakier, like whispers you question hearing, unsure if someone had spoken. This was direct, by a colleague that I had trusted. In that moment, the dynamic changed from the three of us with two clients, to three older men at the table looking at two younger women.

Rachel's extroverted directness saved us with a curt response of "Funny, but let's get down to the details of the meeting."

She was direct enough to let him know that indeed it was not funny and that she wasn't having it, and moved the conversation along. The clients looked awkwardly at us, with faces I couldn't really read. Amusement? Surprise? Professional horror? Rachel transitioned the meeting and took control of what we were going to be doing onsite, and fifteen minutes later we were off to our car to make our way over to the building.

On this trip, we had one rental car for the three of us, for multiple days. As we got into the car, we closed our car doors calmly. Bob was in the driver's seat because you know, the man has to drive, of course.

"Bob, what the hell?" Rachel said. "What the hell was that? You called us girls, and talked about how we were pretty and had to prove that we were smart? To a client?!"

"You can't do that! It is so disrespectful" is what I remember saying, infuriated. I know I had so many other words that I wanted to say and may have, but anger had since blocked them out.

"What? I'm so sorry. I think of you two like my girls, my daughters, and it was a bad joke. I'm so sorry. I didn't mean it like that. It will be fine; they didn't think anything of it." But it wasn't fine. Not for us.

The ride to the client's building was short, so we didn't have a lot of time to deep dive on how wrong this was, and what it meant. Bob would later get to have multiple conversations with us over the next several days on why this was problematic behavior. With one rental car, we were all stuck together to go for dinners and traveling back and forth from the client site for multiple days.

I don't remember going to HR with the incident. Since it happened so early in the trip, we more or less wrote Bob off by the end of it and kept it professional, but nothing more. The client hadn't brought it up, so we returned home and tried to put it behind us. Back in the office, I avoided casual conversations with Bob unrelated to project work.

At one point over a year later, Bob and I got back on track as colleagues, and I agreed to give him feedback on an external project. At this point, the company was going through layoffs. My time came, and I was laid off in the third round of a reduction in force after they lost funding for my position.

It happened very quickly; my manager came in and gave me the news. I asked when my last day would be, thinking it would be at the end of the week. That day was my last day. Even though I had already started looking for other jobs and knew this day would eventually come, my vision was that I would leave for a new job before I was let go. It didn't happen that way. This was an abrupt ending.

It was just like the stereotypical office sitcom, where you see a person packing up a box of their stuff when they've been let go. There I was, trying to awkwardly pack my things, and doing it as quickly as possible. All the while, my remaining coworkers passed my office trying to see what had happened. As I was packing up, Bob walked by and asked, "So will you still help me with my project?"

I stopped what I was doing. *Really? Did he just say that?*

Another female colleague, Stacy, stepped in saying, "Bob, she just lost her job. Leave her alone." Stacy and I weren't super close, but she knew what was happening, and in that moment, she stood up for me. She was the voice that I didn't have.

And no, I did not help Bob with his project.

On another business trip many moons later, in my mid-career, I was in a city that had been on my bucket list to visit for vacation. Even though I was in this tropical location for work, it was still amazing to be there. I was in town to meet with my clients (all male), to work through strategy and goal setting for a new project. On the first night, we had a dinner reservation at sunset at a high-end restaurant with a stunning view of the water. We had cocktails outside on the patio before dinner. Then, we moved inside and were seated at a round table set for six.

One of my clients said, "Laura, you should take this seat so you can see the sunset view over the bay."

I gladly accepted his offer. As I took my seat, the waiter was handing me a menu, and another client, who was seated directly across from me said, "I like this view better."

I looked up at him, and then casually looked behind me to see the view he had. The only thing behind me was the empty foyer of the restaurant. The view he liked so much was of me.

I felt the familiar heat. You know, that heat that you feel as it rises from your gut to your head. I looked down to carefully study what drink I would be having next so that I could avoid eye contact at all costs. I'm one of those people who do not have the right words to say in the moment. I need time to process. I may replay it over again in my head. When I say "may," I mean, I do. I play it back over and over in my head, many times.

Did I hear him right? Did I miss something? Was he talking about something else? Are there flowers behind me? No, the only thing behind me is a door that no one can see through. In that instance I moved on; I said nothing.

If I could go back, I'd say something like, "What, you like looking at [insert name of one of the other men we were eating dinner with]?" or something else that could be seen as humorous, but also snarky enough to let him know that *no dude, that wasn't cool.* Instead, during dinner, I told stories about my amazing husband and beautiful children to make it quite clear that the only view I liked was of the sea and my family.

Several years later, I was in another conference room, in another city, in another meeting. This time, I was one of many women in the room—some clients, some colleagues, and some consultants at various levels in the organization. The conference room over-looked another ocean on another coast. Of course, I was going to take advantage of the view, because I'd be stuck in this conference room for two days, so I staked out a spot where I could take in the panoramic scene. The seats started filling up in our small group meeting, with maybe eight other people in the room besides me. One of our consultants, a man whom I knew well and was more senior than me, put his bag down directly across from me.

He looked directly at me with a smirk and said, "I like my view better than yours." Time slowed down. I felt the familiar heat in my body. I shifted in my seat. I looked up at him with a not-so-happy face. I don't think it was my full-on *WTF or go to hell face, but it wasn't a happy one.*

Other people were still getting settled in, and I wondered if I was the only one who heard him. I was supposed to lead this meeting in just a few minutes; instead, now I was thinking about this comment instead of my actual job of facilitating a strategy session.

I looked down at what I was wearing. I had on a black blouse, black jacket, and cream flowy pants. It was not tight; I was not showing too much skin. It was freezing in the conference room, so I knew to dress for the occasion. That is what I was thinking about. I was questioning my attire, like women are taught to do. I was thinking about how I was going to have to have a conversation with this dude who should totally know better than to say something like that to me. This was what I was thinking about—not thinking about my literal job.

But here's the thing: I'd grown up, gained perspective, and gained experience, which meant as soon as I heard the comment, I immediately knew that I was going to talk to him about it. The statement had crossed a boundary. I knew with certainty that I was willing to have that conversation because I needed to advocate for myself and to ensure that he knew it was not okay to say to me or any other person in the future.

During a break a few hours later, the consultant asked, "Can I talk to you for a minute?"

"Of course," I said. We left the room to chat in the hall.

"Did my comment come off as creepy?" he asked.

"Thank you for initiating this conversation and to ask how it came across. Yes, yes it did." I agreed.

"Okay," he said, "I thought so. I'm sorry; I didn't mean it like that. I say that kind of thing to my daughter and my wife."

I was thinking, *Well, am I your daughter or your wife? No, no I am not. I am someone else's daughter. I am someone else's wife.*

I said, "Well, thank you for having an open conversation about it. That exact comment has been made to me before. It doesn't feel good. I'm glad that we can have an open conversation about how it wasn't appropriate."

He said, "That wasn't my intent."

"Okay," I said, "Thank you for the apology." I wanted the awkwardness to end, so we ended the conversation and went back inside the meeting room.

Hard conversations are awkward. They feel risky to have. In conversations like these, I feel like I need to say the right thing and say it in the right way. In this instance, it was helpful that the consultant had the self-awareness to initiate the conversation. He wanted to get better, to be better. It doesn't make it less awkward, though.

It was hard for me, a people pleaser, to not actively try and make him feel comfortable during the conversation. Even though his comment caused me harm, I was worried about him being comfortable. It is okay to let someone apologize and not absolve them of the harm they caused you. I had to be okay with not placating him or comforting him in that moment, and that was uncomfortable for me to do.

That's the funny thing with power and privilege. He was more senior than I was, and even though he worked at a different company, we still worked together. I didn't want to mess up that relationship. But there is more power in words when they come from people more powerful than you. It is a lesson I think of often, as I am sometimes the most senior person in the room or in the meeting. Your words carry more power. Your actions, too.

It wasn't his intent to cause me harm. Intent doesn't absolve the impact. Impact always wins over intent. Stating the desired intent doesn't lessen the burden on the person that was harmed. It can have the opposing effect. By stating intent, it diminishes the harm caused and centers the conversation back to the person that did the harm. Almost like saying, "Even though you have been harmed by my actions, I didn't mean to, so I'm a good person and you shouldn't feel the feelings that you feel." If you are in the position to be apologizing for your actions, don't talk. Instead, listen. Understand the harm caused.

What I wish he had said: "Laura, I've made you uncomfortable. My comment was inappropriate, and I am so sorry. It will not happen again. I truly value our partnership. What can I do to make amends?"

If he had said that, I think it would have been enough. I don't think there would have been any other actions I needed from him. I would have felt seen and acknowledged.

I learned a lot from this situation, as a leader. It made me think about apologies that I've made in the past. I have used "that wasn't my intent" before in an apology. I'm unlearning and learning. I'll keep trying and will mess up in these conversations, I'm sure of it. But with each conversation, I can get better at advocating for myself and for others around me.

It can be hard to prepare for conflict, but there are some common traps and red flags you can be on the lookout for.

Red Flags and Traps

SOME CALL IT INTUITION, THAT FEELING IN YOUR GUT. If something is wrong, your body has an innate reaction; emotionally and physically, you sense it. You may not be able to stop thinking about it, you may get angry, or feel upset. You need to be able to pay attention to that. That important thing to you might be one of your core values, and you may not be upholding your boundaries (or you may need to put a boundary in place).

How can you be attuned to your values? There will be times when you aren't living your values, when priorities get out of alignment. Find the **Red Flags and Traps Worksheet** in your Values First workbook. Which red flags have you experienced over the last month?

- *Red Flag #1:* Be attuned when your inner warning lights go off. Can you name it? Which core value is it tied to? What is the boundary that you need to put in place?

- *Red Flag #2:* Dreading to have a tough conversation. Adhering to boundaries is hard. You will have to talk about your boundaries often. You may even have to have tough conversations with those that are crossing those boundaries. Tough conversations aren't always fun. If you find yourself dreading having a tough conversation, then that is a red flag and may mean that a boundary has been crossed. Reflect on the situation; which value is coming up for you? Why is that important?

- *Red Flag #3:* Being less excited about a commitment you previously enjoyed. Maybe you did it to help a friend or family member, or you used to love it, but you just don't love it anymore. If you aren't excited about how you are spending your time, then you may need to put in a boundary there and not do that thing anymore.

Sometimes there isn't a warning, and you fall directly into the trap. Below are a few common traps that I've seen leaders fall into time and time again. Use your workbook and the **Red Flags and Traps Worksheet** to identify one trap that you've fallen into in the last month, and what you can do differently going forward.

- *Trap #1: Ruminating.* A trap that can sap your energy or your emotion is ruminating. Some people ruminate or think about something over and over: a meeting that they didn't think went well or a conversation in which they wished they had said something differently. It replays over and over. When I find myself doing this, I take action on something, anything, to get out of the loop and make forward progress. Ruminating about a meeting? I jot down all the things I'm worried about to get them out of my head and make a plan to tackle the things I can control the next day.

- *Trap #2: Adhering to the company culture at your expense.* The culture of an organization is based on what it values. The culture is the written and unwritten rules and behaviors. One trap is to always put the company culture ahead of your own behaviors.

- *Trap #3: Not consistently using systems that support your boundaries.* When you don't use the systems you know that work, it will be harder to uphold your boundaries and live your values.

I gave the example earlier of being in a company culture emphasizing face time when I needed to keep a boundary of family time and have different hours. I fell into that trap for months, even when it was possible to navigate something that would be beneficial to me and still work within the company culture.

In many organizations, there is a "culture of yes"—yes to customers, yes to partners, yes to everything. That can lead to a lot of overburdened and overworked employees. Can you have boundaries within a company that has a "culture of yes"? I think you can. Don't fall into the trap of culture at the expense of your boundaries every time.

We keep a family calendar that integrates my work travel, my husband's work travel, our personal travel, all the kids' appointments and their schedules. It is also where we plan out our dinners for the month. If I don't integrate commitments into the calendar, then something will go awry. We may double book someone or overcommit ourselves. It is a great visual of the weeks to come. It also gives the kids something to look at to let them know what's going on for the week and to set expectations for their days.

Our oldest son started participating in clubs after school on Thursdays when he was seven. He was placed in a yoga class, which was great for him; he was learning how to breathe and do some new stretching poses. On a regular day, he got picked up from school at three. On Thursdays, he got picked up after yoga at four.

We live near the school and can walk there to drop him off. Usually, Brian walked him to school, and our nanny walked to pick him up. One week, my mother came into town to help me because I had been sick earlier in the week, and Brian was traveling for work internationally. It was a normal Thursday. I was working from home and was on Zoom calls all afternoon. Our youngest son was taking an afternoon nap, and my mom was downstairs. Because my mother was visiting, our nanny went home early.

I was on my Zoom call, and I saw a number come through my personal cell phone that I didn't recognize, so I sent it to voicemail. *I'll check it later,* I thought. About twenty minutes later, someone else called on the same number, and it went to voicemail. I checked it to see if I recognized the number, and I didn't. The third time it rang, I excused myself from the meeting and checked the message. It was 3:50 p.m. at this point. I listened to the voicemail, and my heart sank. It was the school calling to ask me when we would be picking up my second-grader. It was Wednesday. It was not Thursday. He was done at three, and I was not there to pick him up. Full-on panic ensued. My stomach dropped.

I fell directly into the trap of not following the systems that support my boundaries. I didn't put it on my calendar. I was minding my own business, being present in my work.

I ended my meeting and RAN to the school. As I sprinted the block and a half, this short distance felt like the farthest that I'd ever experienced as a mother. I ran as fast as I could to go get my baby. As I ran, I tried to call the school back to let them know I'd be there in a minute, but no one answered the phone. I was there within three minutes: 3:53 p.m. I got buzzed into the office.

There he was, bebopping around with his yellow Lego backpack on. He looked at me and said, "Mom, what have you been doing for fifty-three minutes? You are late!"

I grabbed him in the biggest bear hug ever, and I told him, "I mixed up the days and thought it was Thursday, yoga day. I'm so sorry, love." I thanked the school administrator profusely and apologized again. They left at 4:00 p.m. every day. What happened if they couldn't get a hold of you or your emergency contacts? Did they call the police? I have no idea. But I was seven minutes away from that and, oh my God, the guilt.

I'm definitely not living up to my values of family if I'm forgetting to pick up my kid from school. I didn't use the systems that I know work for me. I didn't put it on the calendar. The schedule changed because the variables changed. I didn't adjust and update the calendar.

I know what works: systems to help me put in my boundaries. Use what works. Move on; don't hold on to the guilt. Give yourself grace instead. No ruminating about parent fails. Learn, hug your kiddo, and move on to the next day.

By being aware of the red flags and traps, you can become more attuned to your values and work through conflict faster.

Sometimes we mess up, and we need to do the hard work of being accountable for our actions. I've had to do that many times with my family and colleagues, including once with my team member, Yvonne.

The Highs and Lows of Learning

YVONNE WAS AN AMAZING PRESENTER, FACILITATOR, AND team leader. She was basically a rock star. I was lucky to have her on my team because she was sought out by other leaders often. If there was a new project, they would request Yvonne. If there was a complex problem to solve, was Yvonne available? If there was a hard conversation to have with an external partner, could Yvonne be involved?

Our team had an upcoming meeting, and our senior sponsor of the initiative would kick off the call. Yvonne had spearheaded the work on the project. She built new processes and partnered with multiple departments to get it done. It was a common practice in the company to have a sponsor kick off the call to show support and then hand it over to the team to cover the specifics of the initiative and answer questions.

I had a regular meeting with the senior sponsor and prepped him with talking points while explaining what the session would entail, as one of many action items in our update for the week. I wasn't on the kickoff call because I was leading another meeting at the same time.

After the call, the senior sponsor reached out to me and told me that it had gone well, and that Yvonne had been great, as usual. I pinged Yvonne to tell her about the great feedback from the senior sponsor.

"Interesting," she replied.

"How do you think it went?" I asked.

"It was okay. I will follow up with you later on it."

Uh oh, I thought. Something was off. Yvonne and I were able to catch up at the end of the day on Zoom.

"So how did the meeting go?" I asked.

"He didn't use the bullet points you gave him, like at all." Ugh. We had walked through it together previously, and he hadn't stuck to the messaging when delivering it to the audience.

"What did he say?" I asked, wanting to know all the details.

"He said that the program was part of his strategy from last year."

"Well," I jumped in immediately, "I mean, it is. From his perspective, it does align with his strategy. So, I get where he is coming from. You know him, sometimes he doesn't always stay on topic, even when we give him speaking points," I explained. Yvonne looked defeated. There was a long pause.

"When he described it as part of his strategy, it made me feel like he was taking credit for my work. It was hard on that call. Those were my ideas and my work," Yvonne explained. My heart sank.

"What you just said is hard to hear, too," started Yvonne. There was another long pause—a silence as we both took it in.

"I just did the same thing. Just now, by defending him and explaining it to you."

"Well, yes, yes you did." Another big pause.

"I am so sorry, Yvonne. I should be listening, not explaining. Thank you for sharing your experience with me, and for your honesty. I'm so sorry," I said apologetically. "Do you want me to talk to him about it?"

"No, I don't think so, but let me think about it."

I had let her down. I didn't listen when she was confiding in me. She had trusted me enough to tell me, and then I had caused more harm by explaining why he did what he did. I am so grateful to Yvonne for her leadership, for trusting me and for teaching me. The high point of that conversation was that she trusted me enough to tell me how she felt. The low point was that I wasn't listening to her perspective. I was explaining, not listening.

Through unlearning and relearning through conflict, you may have feelings about the past when you weren't living your own values. Did you do everything you should have done? Did you stand up for this person? Did you give feedback to that horrible boss?

You can't go back. But you can unlearn, relearn, and do better. You can know it isn't always about you. I'm now unlearning many things in my journey into anti-racism—things like centering and intent. We can thank others for teaching us, but it is on us to unlearn. Then to take action. Reading books to bring awareness is a start, but taking the next action is what's best, even when you know you'll do it wrong or get called out. Better to keep learning than not living by the values you know are right. Your discomfort is an easy price to advocate for what's right. Learn, try, do better, repeat.

One of the best ways I've learned to grow from a hard discussion or conflict is through a **High/Low Exercise.** The exercise is a way to learn from situations for continual growth. We are never done learning.

It is essentially an after-action review, or what a project manager may call a postmortem—the meeting you have after a project ends to see what you learned from it. How often do you even have those after-action reviews? Probably not often enough.

Using the **High/Low Exercise** can be beneficial to debrief an individual conflict or a group conflict. I once used it as a way to get a working group back on track.

There was a project team made up of colleagues from multiple departments. Some team members were new, while others had been on the project team for multiple months. We were at a turning point in the project, where some team members wanted to move forward with one solution, and others wanted a different solution. There was also mounting tension, as some members felt like specific team members had hidden agendas, and they had lost trust in them.

I received feedback from a few of the team members and suggested that we all come together as a team to reset expectations. For our kickoff activity, we used the **High/Low Exercise.** We sat around the room at a big oval conference table, and each brought our individual perspectives on the high points of the project to date, the low points, and the impacts at each stage.

As each person presented their experience, every team member listened to differing points of view. Someone's high point for one reason was another's low point for different reasons. A lot was metaphorically put out on the table that day. The walls that some team members had put in place started to crumble, and trust started to build back where the walls once stood. The team agreed to reset and move forward from a place of trust.

Go to the **High/Low Exercise** in your workbook. Think about a situation in which you weren't living your values.

- What was the situation?

- What were the highs of the situation?

- When were you living your values?

- What were the lows of the situation?

- When did you feel at your worst, and what was happening?

- What is your biggest takeaway to live your values more consistently?

By learning from inner and outer conflict, you can learn from your experiences, continue to grow, and do better next time to live in alignment with your values.

By exploring conflict in this section, you learned how to recognize red flags and traps, speak up when you see them, sit with being called out when you miss them, and how to move forward with your values intact when conflict happens.

Next, we will talk about how to sustain your values throughout your lifetime.

Sustaining Values

Sustaining Values

Build an action plan
to live your values
and boundaries for
the long haul.

Values First Framework *from The Catch Group*

Inspiring Lasting Action

YOU'VE FORMED YOUR VALUES FIRST FOUNDATION AND have protected it from threats by building strong boundaries and finding ways to continually grow and evolve from your missteps. In our last part of the Values First Framework, you will build a plan for Sustaining Values.

It has always been inspiring to see people live their values over multiple decades. My dad and paternal grandfather are two such people. My grandfather was an anesthesiologist. Outside of work, he contributed time and money to multiple charitable organizations.

My father followed in his father's footsteps, not as a doctor but as a fundraiser. He built his career in non-profit leadership. Growing up, I have vivid memories of my dad telling me stories about how he would go to various workplaces to encourage employees to contribute to fundraising efforts. He would haul a combination TV/VCR in the back of his white Celebrity station wagon that he would take to early-morning or late-night meetings to show a fundraising video message to employees, to contribute to their company's fundraising goals. Through local fundraising events and actions, the value of advocacy was passed down from father to son.

In the house I grew up in, we had a formal living room and dining room at the front of the house with the nice furniture. You know, the room that kids weren't allowed in, and that was always clean in case we had company come over. My dad would use the dining room as a makeshift office or study space. He would take courses at night to get his MBA. One evening when I was ten or eleven, I remember interrupting him while he was reading a heavy textbook.

"What are you reading, Dad?" I asked.

"Do you want to read the next paragraph?" he asked, moving over so that I could look at the string of words on the big page.

"Um, I can't read that, it is too hard for me."

"Why don't you try?" he asked. I shrugged my shoulders and read a paragraph from his textbook.

"What does that even mean, anyway?" I said, after reading it. He briefly summarized it for me and said, "See, you just read a textbook for MBA students!"

I beamed as he politely guided me out of the room, so I could leave him alone so he could read his book. He studied like that at night for years—six years, to be exact. And we cheered him as he walked across the stage when he got his MBA. At a formal dining room table, the value of growth and development was passed down from father to daughter.

Sometimes values are learned through others close to us. My values of advocacy and growth have been built from my experiences, from seeing it and hearing about it from stories of my grandfather and from seeing it in my father's actions.

It is important to find people in your life, even if you don't directly know them, who inspire you with their values, boundaries, and grace. I am inspired by Betty White for her decades of humor, and Michelle Obama for always going high. Glennon Doyle as an example of evolution and worth, and inner knowing over years of growth. Simone Biles for putting her mental health first, above the expectations of a nation on her Olympic performance. Whether they are mentors we know personally or mentors that we learn from that don't even know we exist, we have a connection to them through their actions, books, podcasts, music, or movies. Seeing others live their values over and over again, over decades, is powerful.

Now it is your turn to reflect on your mentors, those you know personally and those you know from afar. Get out your workbook and turn to your **Values Mentors Worksheet** to reflect on those people who inspire you.

- Whom do you look up to for living their values over time?

- What values have been passed down to you from a family member or friend?

- What family member(s) or friend do you admire for a value that is similar or different from your own?

- What mentors do you follow from afar? Authors, celebrities, philanthropists, musicians, sports legends?

- What ways do you see their values evolve or stay the same?

- What can you learn from them as you think about your own legacy?

Seeing other people live their lives with grace and consistency while putting their values first and keeping their boundaries has inspired me throughout my life and career when I had to make difficult decisions regarding my values.

Evolution through Values

I'D ALWAYS SAY, *I'M NOT AN ENTREPRENEUR.* HECK, I DIDN'T
even like selling Girl Scout cookies growing up. I remember going
door-to-door with my mom and sister. Door-to-door. It gives me
anxiety just thinking about it. Waiting for someone to answer the
door, giving my spiel about Troop #1910 and asking, "Would you
like to buy Girl Scout cookies to support us in our leadership?" I
was competitive, but not so competitive that it outweighed my
true, introverted self. We would go to the houses of my parents'
friends and our neighbors on our street. It was nerve-racking and
anxiety-producing. I hated every minute of it.

The story I've always told myself was that I wasn't entrepreneurial. I've stated that to other humans before—that I'd never
have my own business. That's not me. I'm not a salesperson. I
hate networking. Gouge my eye out with a spork before I'd sign
up for that stuff.

It's funny—the things we tell ourselves, and how those things
usually come true. I'm not a this, I'm not a that…and then you
never are. Self-fulfilling prophecy at its finest.

On my values vision board, I put images and words associated
with my values, a few quotes, and some pictures of family representing my values. While down a rabbit hole on Pinterest one

day, I felt drawn to the quote, "It's not who you are that holds you back, but who you think you're not." I'm not an entrepreneur. I'm not a risk-taker. I'm not a salesperson.

During the search for my next career move, these thoughts held me back because I wasn't entertaining starting my own business as an option. Not at first. As I dissected what I loved to do, coaching came up as something that I knew that I've always loved. You know those days at work when you love your job? That's never been an everyday feeling for me.

Generally, I've had moderately high job satisfaction because I've been learning and growing my career. But the days that I got to coach someone one-on-one, especially in long-term coaching engagements, have always been my favorite days. I remember being excited when I found out we were going to have an internal certification for coaching.

I got certified the next year and dug right in. It brought me so much joy. I got to use data to bring insights to people to improve their performance or impact. We used assessments and qualitative interviews to get data on leaders and how they were being perceived. What were their strengths? What could they do better to make a bigger impact? What business challenges were they facing? Bringing all that data together with their personality picture to give them themes and insights was challenging, and each coaching assignment was different. I was learning a ton.

The first coaching experience I had was for a leader who had worked for the organization for over twenty years. She was an executive in finance. I walked her through her data and asked her questions. She made connections and resonated with some of the feedback. She was truly engaged, and I got to understand more about the business. I brought something to the table that was of interest to her, and I got to know her. She thanked me for the time, and I left thinking *this was a fun day at work. I could do just this,* I thought, *just coaching.*

Well, of course my job wasn't ever just that. I was lucky to have that as part of my job in some capacity in multiple roles over my career. Sometimes I would work with executives for multiple months or a year. Sometimes I would conduct one-time coaching sessions for leaders going through a leadership development program. I was growing myself, as a coach, but also supporting the development of another person in their career.

At a career transition, I thought about what I liked to do and asked myself, *How can I do more of that thing that I like to do? How can I do more coaching?* The first thing that came into my mind was to have my own coaching consultancy. And the second thing that came into my mind was *I'm not an entrepreneur, too risky. I would have to find clients. I'm not a salesperson. I hate selling.* If I thought I couldn't be a coach, then I would never be a coach. What was holding me back was thinking about the things I was "not."

During this time period, I tried to let go of this limiting belief. I started thinking of it as an actual possibility. What would it mean to build a business? What would life look like? I started planning for it at the same time as I was looking for jobs. While I was interviewing, I was also building out a business plan for my own company. It was liberating. I knew more than I thought I did. My experience would be valuable to others. It was not if, but when, I would start my own coaching practice.

In the midst of the pandemic in my mid-career, leading my team through change, I felt a tugging. At first it was a slight tap, like a nudge. Work seemed harder. Getting through each day felt more exhausting. We were in the middle of a pandemic. The kids were still in virtual school, and we were still home most of the time. *I'm exhausted by this new normal,* I thought.

On my walks, I was being drawn towards listening more to entrepreneurial podcasts, and less to my beloved true crime podcasts. It was interesting to hear about how others were scaling online businesses, about email-list building, and building a brand. The nudge became more frequent.

The exhaustion of the everyday compounded for me, like it did for everyone during this time. I did my best to separate that feeling from my "work self"—you know, the self that shows up at work, even when you are exhausted, mad, frustrated, etc. But I'm a horrible poker player. I wear my heart and my emotions on my face. My team knew I wasn't myself, and I tried to be as open as possible without putting more burden on them. I was exhausted, and rationalized that the exhaustion was okay and that it would get better.

I kept going like this for months, with the nudges showing up through journaling (something I had picked up doing as part of my pandemic ritual). I'd find myself writing more and more about what could be, and how I wanted to impact the world. I was becoming more centered in journaling, connecting myself back to my values.

Was it that I was exhausted because of everything? Or was it that and something else? What did I feel connected to? What did I not feel connected to?

Until one day, the nudge became a push.

I asked my husband, "Just because I can do a job, should I do a job?"

I already knew the answer to this question.

He did too, and asked supportively, "What do you want to do?"

"Coach women to get into bigger jobs and make an impact." The answer fell out of my mouth as quickly and as matter-of-factly as if someone asked me what time it was.

"Then let's figure out how you can do that," said Brian, without skipping a beat.

I knew that I'd wanted to go in this direction eventually—eventually, you know, after I'd accomplished everything I'd wanted to in this job or that job, for this organization or for that organization. But I didn't want to leave my team. I didn't want to leave a great organization where there was so much potential for me to make an impact.

In his book, *The Surprising Power of Not Knowing What to Do,* Jay Cone, PhD, describes that in self-reflection, we need to be aware of our own frames of reference, assumptions, and counter-productive assumptions.[12] He goes on to describe competing commitments. I felt like I had competing commitments. A commitment to my team and organization. Another commitment to myself and my values.

In my exhaustion, I realized that I was trying to live two competing truths. The first truth was to be in a job I mostly loved with an amazing team. The second was building a business that aligned with my values of growth, development, and advocacy to help more women get into top jobs and lead as their authentic selves. I couldn't do both at the same time. That wouldn't be fair to the organization I worked for, my team, my family, or me. I had to give up one of those things.

The push towards my values was more, it was bigger. I needed to make a decision.

Wrong, I needed to make a plan to go along with the decision that I'd already made. I needed to run towards my values. I needed to leave my job and start coaching women.

The push turned into a leap. I left my C-suite job in the middle of a pandemic. I transitioned to building a coaching firm. Within two months of leaving my job, I'd launched the company, The Catch Group, and my podcast called *You Belong in the C-Suite*. The anxiety-ridden girl that hated selling Girl Scout cookies was now a founder of a company. The nervous grad student with a white Banana Republic jacket at a job fair was now getting other women into top jobs. The introverted woman who didn't give her opinions at the boardroom table was now a podcast host bringing her voice into the world.

To be the leader that I needed to be for myself and others, I needed to continue to show up through my values. I needed a plan for sustainability. So do you.

Your Values First Action Plan

TO BUILD YOUR SUSTAINABLE PLAN, YOU'LL USE THE worksheets and exercises that you've been using throughout this book. You'll set aside time for intentional self-reflection every ninety days. You'll also have your workbook at the ready for the just-in-time learning and reflection moments.

Let's build your action plan. Go to your workbook (available at www.thecatchgroup.com/valuesfirst) to fill out your **Values First Action Plan** to act on what matters most. Below is a recommended approach to setting up your action plan to sustain your values and boundaries.

Enlist a partner from your Catch Crew and set up a time to build your action plan together. Create a tradition of an annual review with quarterly checkpoints, and go over the topics below with your Catch Crew.

To start, schedule an annual review with your Catch Crew. Schedule a time where you can get together with one or a few peers and set yourselves up for successfully living your values-first priorities.

Want to broaden your Catch Crew, or accelerate your development? Consider joining our community or group coaching programs for accountability and mentorship (learn more at www. thecatchgroup.com/valuesfirst).

Annual Catch Crew Check-in

- Start your plan off right with your **Values Check-in Worksheet.** Check in with your values; are they still the right ones? How are you feeling about them?

- Audit Time and see where your values are showing up in your life with the **Calendar Review Worksheet.** I love to do a beginning-of-the-year reflection and audit how I'm spending my time.

- Check in on your boundaries. Are you celebrating your boundaries consistently? Do you need to set a new boundary?

- How are you Uplifting Others? How are you supporting your Catch Crew? Do you need support in new areas? How are your values showing up at work with your team? What actions do you need to take on building the culture from your **Culture Builder Worksheet?**

- Before you leave, schedule your next check-in with your Catch Crew.

Ninety-Day Catch Crew Check-in

- Complete and review your **Values Check-in Worksheet.** Questions to ask your Catch Crew for accountability:

- Did anything change in your core values after your Values Check-in?

- Last time you were working on prioritizing this core value and had this boundary. How is it going?

- What did you do to celebrate your success?

- How have your values been showing up consistently at work?

- What modeling have you done for your team? What is resonating with them?

- When should we check in again?

Remember everything that you have in your workbook at your disposal for when you need it. Review your Values First Toolkit at the end of the book as a reminder of how and when to use the tools you've learned.

You now have a plan for sustaining your values that includes inspirational mentors, room for evolution, and a toolkit for upholding your values and fortifying your boundaries.

Conclusion

YOU DID IT; YOU'VE BUILT YOUR VALUES FIRST LIFE THROUGH a lot of self-reflection and taking action.

This isn't a one-and-done kind of thing. The Values First Framework and the tools that you've used can be used throughout the course of your career and life. I hope that you revisit your values often and create boundaries that enable you to live the life and career you want. I hope you lead as your authentic self and model behaviors you want to see to empower others to do the same.

The world needs more diversity and authenticity in the workforce. Most importantly, that includes your leadership.

Let's summarize the journey you've been on:

Values First. You identified your core values and set your foundation. You named what's most important to you and defined what living those values means.

Audit Time. You checked in with your values to make difficult decisions and reviewed your calendar to see where your values are showing up. You prioritized what is most important.

Life Boundaries. You tied your boundaries to a value as a motivation to help you keep them. You learned a three-step process to set, keep, and celebrate your boundaries with grace and consistency.

Uplifting Others. You built your Catch Crew, know the importance of supporting each other to live your values, and understand how to build a culture to inspire your team from your values.

Experiencing Conflict. You worked through your red flags and traps and learned how to grow and move forward when conflict happens.

Sustaining Values. You know whom to look up to for inspiration in living a life tied to your values and have built a plan for sustaining action with your many tools to help you along the way.

Your values are your foundation. Use your values to set boundaries to live a life around your values. Use your values and your boundaries to make the everyday decisions, have the difficult conversations, and make the difficult decisions.

Your leadership belongs in the places that you are and the places you seek to be in. Live a life tied to your values, keep your boundaries, and model that to empower the same for others.

Ground yourself in your values first. And do it with gravitas.

Values First Toolkit

Values Worksheet—to gain clarity on what matters most. Use this annually to gain clarity and ground yourself in your values. This is your foundation.

Values Check-in—to revisit your values and check in on how you are feeling about them showing up in your life. Use this quarterly and chat with a Catch Crew partner afterwards.

I'm Living My Values When Worksheet—to identify what success looks like when you are living your values. Review this to prioritize boundaries you need to build. Get this out when you have a big boundary to build (e.g., decision about a new job).

Values Vision Board—as a physical reminder of your values. Display this on your desk as a reminder of what you aspire to.

Values Calendar Review—to audit your calendar to find out how you are spending your time and if your values are showing up in your life.

Life Boundary Builder—to prioritize boundaries aligned with your values, set up a system, and celebrate your consistency. Use this when you have a new boundary that you need to build or tweak a previous one.

My Catch Crew Worksheet—to identify whom you support and who supports you. Your peers can be great accountability partners on your journey. Review this tool annually.

Culture Builder Worksheet—to make a plan of action to uplift others. You are a leader and have influence. Model your boundaries for others, especially at work. Use this worksheet with your team to create the culture that aligns with their values.

Red Flags and Traps Worksheet—as a reminder of what to avoid and what boundaries you may need to put in place.

High/Low Worksheet—to debrief a tough situation individually or with a team. Use this often and continually learn and grow.

Values Mentors Worksheet—to get inspiration from others as you sustain your values throughout your life. Add new mentors to your list as you meet them and learn from them.

Values First Action Plan—to take sustainable action and live a values-first life.

V	**A**	**L**	**U**	**E**	**S**
Values First	Audit Time	Life Boundaries	Uplifting Others	Experiencing Conflict	Sustaining Values
Dig into what matters most to you, and set the foundation of your core values. You'll also get clarity on what living those values looks like uniquely to you.	Review your time to see where your values do and don't show up in your life, and learn how to use your values to make difficult decisions at home and work.	Set your Values First priorities to create the boundaries you need to truly live the life that you want, and create a system for keeping those boundaries in place.	Find the support you need from peers and mentors to keep your boundaries intact, and learn strategies to model your values with your team by building a Values First culture as a leader.	Create a plan now so when conflict arises with yourself or your team, you can easily know what to avoid and how to move forward in alignment with your values.	Build an action plan to live your values and boundaries for the long haul.

Values First Framework *from The Catch Group*

To get the free Values First workbook, go to thecatchgroup. com/valuesfirst, to take action on what matters most.

Acknowledgments

I'M SO GRATEFUL TO HAVE A LIFE FULL OF PEOPLE WHO LOVE and support me.

To my husband, Brian, for being my biggest supporter. Thank you for always believing in me, for relentlessly supporting my goals (there are a lot of them), and for loving me no matter what.

To my boys, thank you for always wanting to listen to Mommy's stories, for being patient when I was writing, and for asking how my writing and coaching is going. You are both the best.

To my parents, who were my teachers throughout my life through their values, experiences, and examples. I love you.

Lauren, the best editor and book coach, thank you. You pushed me to get this book out into the world. Your process helped me write it, and your editing brought it to life. You were the first one to get me to see that I was a writer, not just someone randomly journaling through a pandemic. I'm so grateful to have you as mentor and friend.

Thank you to the WYFBA writing community, especially to Stephanie and Paige, who have read many versions of this book. So many writing Zoom sessions, so many memories.

To Arlene, my mentor, friend, and fellow author. Thank you for making this book better.

To Maddy, for your perspective and positivity. You helped shape the very early stages of this book without realizing it.

To Renae, for strategizing with me, supporting me, and pushing me to put my resume in the box to start my company.

To my publishing team, you are amazing at what you do and smoothly guided me through this process.

To my clients who inspire me daily, you are making huge impacts in the world, and you are doing it by living your values.

To friends, family, colleagues, and team members who have inspired me to lead and live a life guided by my values, I cannot thank you enough.

References

1 Siegel, Daniel, and Tina Payn Bryson. 2012. *The Whole-Brain Child: 12 Revolutionary Strategies to Nurture Your Child's Developing Mind*. New York: Bantam.

2 Lexico, s.v. "core value,". 2021. *Lexico*. https://www.lexico.com/definition/core_value.

3 David, Susan, interview by Brené Brown, 2016. *Emotional Agility: Get Unstuck, Embrace Change and Thrive in Work and Life*. London: Penguin.

4 David, Susan, interview by Brené Brown. 2021, March 8. *Brené with Dr. Susan David on The Dangers of Toxic Positivity,* Part 2 of 2.

5 *Merriam-Webster*. 2021. https://www.merriam-webster.com/dictionary/gravitas.

6 Helgesen, Sally, and Marshall Goldsmith. 2018. *How Women Rise: Break the 12 Habits Holding You Back from Your Next Raise, Promotion, or Job*. New York: Penguin Random House.

7   Mohr, Tara Sophia. 2014, August 25. hbr.org. https://hbr.org/2014/08/why-women-dont-apply-for-jobs-unless-theyre-100-qualified.

8   Nagoski, Emily, and Amelia Nagoski. 2020. *Burnout: The Secret to Unlocking the Stress Cycle.* New York: Ballantine Books.

9   Mihalich-Levin, Lori. 2021. *Logging Back on at Night (a.k.a. the Split Shift). Mindful Return.* https://www.mindfulreturn.com/split-shift.

10 McGinty, Jo Craven. 2020, October 30. "With No Commute, Americans Simply Worked More During Coronavirus." *The Wall Street Journal.* https://www.wsj.com/articles/with-no-commute-americans-simply-worked-more-during-coronavirus-11604050200.

11 Mann, Annamaria. 2021, January 15. "Why We Need Best Friends at Work" *Gallup, Inc.* https://www.gallup.com/workplace/236213/why-need-best-friends-work.aspx.

12 Cone, Jay Gordon. 2021. *The Surprising Power of Not Knowing What to Do: Discovering Creativity and Compassion in a Time of Chaos. Unstuck Minds Media.*

Made in the USA
Coppell, TX
13 April 2022

76502186R00111